A COMPLETE SYSTEM FOR THE TOURNAMENT BRIDGE PLAYER

Tuğrul Kaban

An Honors Book from Master Point Press

Honors Books is an imprint of Master Point Press. All contents,
editing and design (excluding cover design) are the sole
responsibility of the authors.

Master Point Press
214 Merton St. Suite 205
Toronto, Ontario, Canada
M4S 1A6
(647) 956-4933

info@masterpointpress.com

www.masterpointpress.com
www.bridgeblogging.com
www.teachbridge.com
www.ebooksbridge.com

ISBN: 978-1-77140-156-2

Cover Design: Olena S. Sullivan/New Mediatrix

1 2 3 4 5 6   19 18 17 16

Contents

Introduction

This book is intended as a ready-made practical full system for the tournament bridge player. It also lends itself to good use by a partnership wanting to experiment with some new ideas which they can take up with little additional discussion and no further research.

The book does not try to teach you how to play bridge. All that is taken for granted. Rather, you are presented with a full selection of conventions that cover all practical aspects of bidding and carding. There is no claim that this is necessarily the "best" collection of all possible conventions. But it is a thought-through and tried-and-tested set of conventions which sit comfortably within the book's basic system choice of strong no-trump and 5-card majors in a 2-over-1 game-force setting.

Each part of the system is explained in turn in the book and the appendix contains ready-made conventions cards (WBF, ACBL and EBU versions) together with 20-page supplementary notes. These notes also serve as a handy summary of the entire system discussed in the book.

Some of the conventions I suggest are a little outside the mainstream, such as Muiderberg, Rubensohl, Questem, to name a few. How about playing Puppet-Stayman not just over 2NT but also over 1NT? Many players will have come across these before although they may not have experimented with them personally. There is a certain consistency of the chosen conventions with each other and also with the overall system.

The more common conventions in the system are not explained but presumed, although I sometimes like to change some aspect or invert some meaning, in which case these are fully reasoned. Notwithstanding my minor changes to the better known conventions I owe them all to their original creators, far too many to mention by name and far too great to need my acknowledgement here.

There are also some methods in the book that are my own creations for the most part which I have been quietly playing to good effect for many years. These include my version of transfer responses to a 1♣ opening (which have a different approach than most other transfer schemes in this area) and my structure for overcalling opponents' 1NT (which caters for having one or both majors and at the same time distinguishes between weak, intermediate or strong overcalls).

I also have some definite preferences which diverge from standard-American. For example, 1♣ in this book promises only 2 cards in the suit (and 1♦ shows 4+ cards), with the rebid usually clarifying the hand pattern. The idea of a 1NT-opener containing a 5-card major may also be anathema to some old-timers, but it is not so unusual anymore.

There are many useful smaller tools and gadgets in the book. For example: composite negative doubles and support doubles (depending on claims on the majors by either side in the prior bidding); switched meanings of pass and double when opponents cue-bid our suit (so we don't give them additional bidding space); stopper-showing passes when opponents double our artificial bids (and how we reconvene our sequence); and a lot of transfer-bidding (not just in response to 1♣ opening but also when our 1M opening is doubled and after partner overcalls opponents' opening bid). These are all very user-friendly and extremely effective tools in competitive situations.

Indeed I hope that you will find the whole book user-friendly and readily adoptable with your willing partner. And finally, in the book's bidding sequences the opener is a 'she' and the responder a 'he'. This is not just my small contribution to gender balance in the use of language but also a practical way to differentiate between the two hands during the rest of the bidding and commentary.

Tuğrul Kaban

September 2015

Acknowledgements

I owe a debt of gratitude to Stuart Brown. my brother-in-law. who introduced me to bridge when I was 16. That introduction duly took care of my last couple of years at school in Turkey and all my years at university in the UK. I then took a complete break of 17 years from the game for family and work reasons but returned with a vengeance in 1998 since when I have been fortunate to have a succession of some great partners.

Notable among them are Barry Davies. 27 years my senior. with whom I played until 2003 and who sadly passed away since then: then Andrew Lee. my contemporary in age and an uncanny likeness of bridge mind. who unfortunately had to discontinue competitive bridge for medical reasons in 2010; and latterly Tom Dessain. 27 years my junior. who undoubtedly has a great bridge life ahead of him at the top level well beyond my remaining years. Andrew and Tom selflessly tried and tested all my unusual system ideas with me over the years and at times contributed some of their own to the full system in this book.

I would not have been able to spend anything like as much time on my bridge without the patience and encouragement of my better-half, Catherine, herself no bridge player. But I was delighted when my daughter Rosa took up the game at university and has since been playing regularly.

Both Rosa and Tom enthusiastically proofread the book for my English as well as its bridge content but any residual errors remain all mine. Credit is due to Tom also for reformatting the book into its present final shape.

Tuğrul Kaban

September 2015

Chapter 1

Choice of Basic System

There are many basic systems in the bridge playing world which significantly differ in their approach to bidding. Some older systems have gradually been supplemented if not entirely replaced by their modern day equivalents over the years. The second half of the 20th Century also witnessed a fair amount of artificial systems developing.

Once upon a time Charles Goren's methods ruled the world (16-18 HCP no-trump, 5-card majors), with the notable exception of Acol prevalent in some parts (12-14 HCP no-trump, 4-card majors). The latter is still going strong in Britain today although it looks a little neglected, Albert Benjamin's 2-bids being its last significant update a long time ago and Eric Crowhurst's Acol Index being the only major attempt to codify it.

But the former changed not only its no-trump range to 15-17 HCP in becoming the Standard-American but also added layers to the depth

and sophistication of its still fairly natural bidding methods over
the decades and in so doing became more like the world standard.
So much so that in large parts of the world today and not just in
North America. bridge players refer to it simply as *the* standard - a
deserving shorthand of its full name.

1.1   Artificial systems

As for artificial bidding systems. the most enduring has been the
Precision Club. It has a small but dedicated following in most
places and it is in fact more like the norm in some parts of Eastern
Europe such as Bulgaria. Multiple world champions Eric Rodwell
and Jeff Meckstroth of USA are a testament to the durability of
this artificial system although Meckwell play their own particular
variant of Precision.

Some other systems are artificial only to the extent of certain
multiple-meaning bids or that their popularity seems mostly
geographical. Polish Club. for example. has near-total following in
Poland but a limited take-up elsewhere. At times this can be a
matter of strength for the system. The small nation of Iceland won
the World Championships in 1991 thanks in no small measure to
its Icelandic Club system.

Historically. though. Roman Club of the 1950s must have the
biggest claim to success among artificial systems considering that it
helped the Italian Blue Team to 12 World Team Championships. 3
Olympiads and numerous European and national titles.

Notable among the 21st Century hybrid systems is Fantunes. the

system played by the world's 1st and 2nd ranked players Fulvio
Fantoni and Clauido Nunes who represented Italy at the highest
level for many years before being recruited to Monaco more
recently. Fantunes have few followers yet but a few more books on
it will no doubt remedy that in time.

An element of artificiality is surely no bad thing. It can inject more
science and fun into the game. However, purely artificial methods
are not without danger either; when something goes astray in a relay
sequence the two halves of a partnership may well end up with two
very different scenarios of the bidding with disastrous consequences.

1.2   The future

What of the future? I believe that generally natural systems will
continue to dominate. There will of course be an increasing amount
of specialised undertones creeping into natural systems which will
subvert them somewhat in the direction of artificial bidding. But,
notwithstanding that arbitrary dose of artificial bidding in anyone's
system. the fundamentals for most bridge players - their basic
system - will no doubt remain firmly rooted in the realms of
primarily natural bidding.

After all. newcomers to the game start inevitably with natural
systems. And most will continue so. Adding complications to the
system is not everyone's favourite pastime. It requires additional
effort and time. which some would rather spend on actually playing
the game as it comes. If it comes with any sense of completeness so
much the better.

That's where the strength of the North-American system lies - it does rather come as a fairly complete system with a standardised set of understandings. Whilst there is no bar to plurality in the game, the fact of broad convergence of methods or rather the dominance of one over the others - irrespective of their origin - can actually benefit the game. It becomes easier for bridge players from different parts of the world to share their game.

The simplicity of the North-American system also makes its spread easier if not inevitable. It is not surprising, for example, that as the take-up of bridge gathers pace in China and other parts of the Far East, they are looking no further than Standard-American or its update, the 2-over-1.

Indeed all swaths of bridge playing fraternities seem to know only of these methods. Turkey, a keen card-playing nation, swears by the 2-over-1 methods to the extent that if you do anything else they assume that what you have done was wrong, not different.

It is also no coincidence that the online bridge community is overwhelmingly playing the 'standard' or 2-over-1 methods. On some sites it seems pretty much exclusively so. Online it is especially important that people can start playing with little or no discussion and those methods fit well in those circumstances. This won't provide the higher level partnership understanding you would like but it is often adequate for a quick fix of a game.

The other reason for the popularity of the 'standard' methods and especially the 2-over-1 system is that these lend themselves better to IMP-scoring. IMP-scoring is no longer the measure just for the teams format; it is also the scoring method of choice for the pairs game especially in North America whereas matchpoints remain firmly the rule for the pairs format in Europe. It is not a coincidence that

opponents with lesser hands do not intervene as much when playing
under IMP conditions and this benefits systems such as the 2-over-1
system which relies on a free ride in the bidding. 2-over-1 methods
of course revert to standard methods if the first opponent intervenes
over our opening bid.

1.3   A solid basic system

Acol players seem to need a lot of time to discuss systems before
they can have a game. There is relatively little that is unarguably
standard in Acol. Each aspect needs to be touched on and very little
can be presumed. Not even the no-trump range anymore. 2-level
bids certainly needs discussion specifically, even if only to decide on
Benji or reverse-Benji, or maybe even multi-2♦. Will jump overcalls
be weak or intermediate, or depend on vulnerability? How do we
escape when our weak no-trump is doubled? And so on.

By contrast, Standard-American comes ready-made with a lot more
default assumptions and understandings. No wonder people can even
play 'standard' with pick-up partners (and professionals) that they
meet (engage) on their way into the playing room in tournaments.
The SAYC seems to have dealt with most of it and you can presume.

The choice of the basic system is important - before I present my
choice of conventions and gadgets, which are what this book is really
about. The latter will sit within the basic system that is decided first
and will also provide the default framework.

From all that I have said above, you will not be surprised to see me
conclude that, in my opinion, natural systems will naturally remain

the bedrock of bridge bidding and among them Standard-American stands out, except only that its new extension, the 2-over-1 game-force methods, are gradually superseding Standard-American itself.

That is, therefore, my choice of basic system on which the rest of my methods are built. Before we discuss the rest, let's first go over the basic system itself, so that's what I turn to next.

Chapter 2

2/1 Game Force

The 2-over-1 game-force response system is increasingly the predominant bidding system in the world. It is based on Standard American with 5-card majors and strong no-trump but its adherents scc it almost as an entirely different system in its own right. The main difference is in the meanings of 2-level responses to a major-suit opening.

If responder's first bid is 2 of a lower-ranking new suit, it sets up a forcing auction which cannot rest below game-level. This is the general idea - with one significant exception which is that if responder repeats his minor suit then the sequence becomes invitational only (this is the Mike Lawrence version of 2-over-1).

The superiority of the 2-over-1 system is that it saves bidding space. Having made a 2-level response initially, responder doesn't have to jump anymore to show game-forcing values. Because the auction can stay low, we have more room to exchange information and even explore slam possibilities below the game level.

One of the drawbacks of reserving 2-over-1 responses to game-going hands is that the same response can no longer encompass invitational hands of 10-11 HCP. The latter are now covered by the Forcing No-Trump response, another key feature of the 2-over-1 system which, as we will see in Chapter 3, now shows a 6-11 HCP range and denies game-forcing values but usually forces one more round of bidding to identify the best contract.

2.1   Main principles

A 2-over-1 bid by responder is forcing-to-game only when our side opens the bidding in a major in 1st or 2nd seat and the first opponent passes.

If the first opponent overcalls or doubles, the system no longer applies in the same way and responder's bids now revert to the partnership's otherwise agreed methods.

Naturally the system also does not apply when our side opens in 3rd or 4th seat. This is because here responder, now a passed hand, is obviously not in a position to unconditionally force to game.

In effect the only sequences where 2-over-1 game-force applies are the following 5 sequences:

1♥-2♣, 1♥-2♦, 1♠-2♣, 1♠-2♦, 1♠-2♥

A 2-over-1 response is not mandatory to show game values. Responder is free to make another start to the bidding if some other bid is more appropriate because playing the 2-over-1 system does not affect the meanings of other auctions.

Thus, 1-level responses (1♥-1♠), direct raises of partner's suit (whether single raise or pre-emptive), systematic raises (such as Bergen raises or Jacoby 2NT), or other agreements (for example weak jump shifts or splinter bids), in other words the rest of your system still equally apply alongside the 2-over-1 forcing-to-game responses. The only exception is the 1NT response which now has a slightly different meaning.

Opener's rebid in 2-over-1 sequences is often a rebid of the same suit (1♥-2♦-2♥). This does not guarantee a 6+ card suit. A range of other possible bids by opener have specific meanings and a simple rebid in the same suit only says that it was not appropriate to make some other specific new bid. There is of course no danger of it being passed out.

It follows that where there is scope opener will rebid more strongly and bypass the original suit to show some extra values or features. A 2-level reverse rebid (1♥-2♣-2♠) shows extra values but not necessarily a great deal more; 15+ HCP is good enough for a reverse after responder's 2/1.

Similarly opener's high-level reverse rebid (3 of a new lower-ranking suit) shows some extra values; again 15+ HCP is fine after responder's 2/1.

The system is geared primarily to making the most of major suit fits, especially 5-3 fits.

2.2   Responder's minor-suited hands

Of course responder will be dealt his fair share of minor suit hands
as well but he is equally well equipped in a 2-over-1 environment to
bid those out too.

Although a response of 2♣ or 2♦ to 1M is initially also forcing to
game, the difference with minor suit hands is that responder can
backtrack a little by repeating his minor suit.

This exception to the system means that responder can start with an
initial 2-over-1 response in a minor suit when holding no more than
around 10-11 HCP and a 6+ card suit. His 3-level rebid in the minor
will complete the message and re-define the hand as invitational only.
So it is possible that the bidding may subside below game after all
unless of course opener has extras.

Opener's raise of responder's minor in the first place (1♥-2♣-3♣)
also shows some extras on her part so an invitational responder in
that situation is entitled to make another move.

If opener's rebid was 2NT (a two way bid, either 12-14 or 18-19
HCP) then a responder with an invitational minor suit hand will
still simply rebid his minor, presuming opener to have only 12-14
HCP. But if opener has the 18-19 HCP hand type instead then she
will continue bidding over responder's 3m and so game will still be
reached.

A 1♦-2♣ start is also forcing initially but not necessarily all the way
to the 5-level in either minor. More specifically 1♦-2♣-2♦-3♣ (10-11
HCP, 6+ clubs) is also invitational, rather like when opener starts

with a major. If partner opens 1♦ and you hold invitational strength with only five clubs, a jump to 2NT (via 2♠ if playing transfers) is a better move as your first response.

2.3 Responder's first bid in a 2/1 environment

After that detour about minor-suit hands let's get back on track with all our bidding options in a 2-over-1 setting and take each round of bidding in turn, once partner opens one of a major.

Responder's first priority is to announce any immediate fit with opener's major. So, make the appropriate direct or systemic raise of partner's major if you have 4-card support - a single, limit, pre-emptive, forcing or splinter raise, depending on your strength and shape. I prefer a single raise with all 3-card fits in the more traditional 6-9 HCP range (rather than some of the lesser hands in that range going through a forcing 1NT response as in some 2-over-1 versions).

In the absence of a fit with partner's major, the next best thing at the 1-level is the other major if you have it (that is, respond 1♠ to a 1♥ opening).

Failing those but otherwise still with values to force to game, our 2-over-1 system comes into its own by enabling you to spell out your game intention with a simple response in a new suit at the 2-level. A game force is usually 12+ HCP but it should be interpreted as any hand with which you would have opened the bidding or a hand that becomes worth upgrading with some degree of fit with partner's opening suit.

After partner opens 1 of a major, a 2♣ or 2♦ response shows a 4+ card suit. Initially it denies a fit for opener's major, although later bids might show a temporarily concealed three-card fit. In rare cases, a 2♣ initial response may be a 3-card suit, such as with a 3-4-3-3 shape facing a 1♠ opening.

A 2♥ response to opener's 1♠ promises a 5+ card suit as usual. Initially it denies a fit for opener's major, although later bids might show a temporarily concealed three-card fit.

Of course you can also respond at 2-level in a minor with only 10-11 HCP and a 6+ card suit as we already discussed, subject to re-defining the hand as invitational with your next bid.

Last but not least, with all other unpassed hands in the 6-11 HCP range including invitational hands with or without 3-card support for opener's major, you can respond initially with a wide range 1NT. We will discuss this 1NT response in Chapter 3.

2.4   Opener's second bid

There is a school of thought about 2-over-1 auctions that after the initial forcing-to-game response neither partner has to jump to show extra values. Conversely, there are also those in the 2-over-1 world who subscribe to the view that opener can even reverse with no extra values over any reply. I don't believe either of these strategies works well.

A better approach is that responder does not jump with strong hands, but opener does.

In most 2-over-1 auctions, responder is in charge because he has more information about opener's hand than opener has about responder's. When responder has a strong hand, he chooses forcing, low-level rebids to give opener maximum room to provide more information. Responder tends to do the asking and opener the telling.

If in these situations opener were to bid both weak and strong hands in the same way, responder would never be able to make an intelligent decision about how far to go.

It follows that it is important for opener to communicate her strength as early as possible in the auction. To do this, opener makes value bids that show whether she has a minimum hand or has extras - she bids less with less, and more with more. Opener will also be more restrained about upgrading her hand for ruffing values because those tend be more valuable in responder's hand with the shorter trump suit.

Opener's options for her second bid after responder's 2-over-1 response are, more specifically, as follows:

With a minimum hand (12-14 HCP), opener makes a simple rebid in the same suit or in a lower-ranking suit or in no-trumps (1♥-2♣-2♥ or 2♦ or 2NT). Jumping to game in your own suit is also minimum but with a long, good suit (1♥-2♦-4♥).

Rebidding your major does not necessarily show a 6-card suit. The hand may simply be unsuitable for a no-trump rebid because of particular weakness in a suit or a new suit bid may not be appropriate because of the relative rank of the second suit. So, facing a forcing 2-over-1 response, a simple rebid by opener in a major on 5 cards is not uncommon.

With some extra values or shape (15+ HCP), opener needs to announce this by making a jump (1♥-2♣-3♥ or 3NT), a reverse bid (1♥-2♣-2♠), a high reverse (1♥-2♦-3♣), a raise of responder's suit (1♥-2♦-3♦), a splinter in support of responder's suit (1♥-2♦-3♠ or 4♣), or a minor-suit RKCB enquiry for responder's minor (1♥-2♦-4♦).

Facing a 2-over-1 response, the only strong hand which opener does not reveal immediately is a balanced 18-19 HCP hand type because here opener rebids 2NT as a dual range rebid with 12-14 or 18-19 HCP. Responder nevertheless would not pass this 2NT even if his earlier 2-over-1 was based on a 10-11 HCP minor suit invitational hand. If responder bids 3NT then opener still shows her extra strength by a raise (1♥-2♣-2NT-3NT-4NT).

I defined extra values as 15+ HCP but of course these opener hands would exclude most 15-17 HCP balanced hand types with which we would have opened 1NT even when holding a 5-card major. So when opener's rebid indicates extras she will have either more shape or more points or possibly both.

2.5   Responder's second bid

The rationale of the system is that responder goes slowly when he has extra values but uses the fast-arrival principle when he has a minimum hand. This is particularly relevant to responder's second bid.

A return to opener's suit at the lowest level (1♠-2♣-2NT-3♠, i.e. slow) indicates some extra values (14+ points) and gives opener more room to describe her hand. On the other hand, a jump to game in opener's suit (1♠-2♣-2NT-4♠, i.e. fast) shows a minimum hand (12-13 points) and denies interest in slam. In both these sequences responder is marked with 3-card support. Indeed, responder is marked with a 3-card fit most of the time he gives belated support.

A rebid of 2NT (1♥-2♦-2♥-2NT) is still unlimited, probably with stoppers in the other suits, enabling opener room to describe her hand further.

A repeat of a minor suit (1♥-2♦-2♥-3♦) is the usual way for responder to backtrack on the game-force and instead reveal only an invitational hand with a 6+ card minor suit.

A new suit (1♥-2♦-2♥-2♠ or 3♣) may not always be a 4-card suit but is still a forward move with an unlimited hand. Notice how it again provides room for opener to further describe her hand.

However, an unneccesary jump in a new suit when a non-jump bid in that suit would have been still forcing, is now a shortage, agreeing opener's last bid suit and forcing. Responder will have a 3-card fit if opener was rebidding a major (1♥-2♦-2♥-3♠ or 4♣) but 4-card support if it was opener's second suit (1♥-2♣-2♦-3♠).

A second round jump to 4NT by responder would be RKCB for opener's last/second suit (1♥-2♣-2♦-4NT) or quantitative if opener's last bid was 2NT (1♥-2♦-2NT-4NT).

2.6   Opener's third bid

By this time a lot of information will have already been exchanged in addition to the agreement in the first place that the bidding will not stop below game level. Opener's third round bid tends to be either an answer to responder's call for more information in the absence of a fit, or a decision whether to investigate slam prospects below game level if suit agreement had already been reached.

If responder has made a bid that asks for more information (1♥-2♦-2♥-2♠ or 2NT or 3♣) that would have also meant that he does not have 3-card support for opener's suit. In that case it is incumbent on our opener to make a clarifying bid to enable responder to choose the right contract.

A repeat by opener of her suit at the lowest level (3♥) here would confirm a good 6-card suit (remember that the earlier 2♥ rebid did not guarantee 6), whereas a jump to 4♥ would show a good but typically not solid 7+ card suit.

The next best thing opener can reveal is 3-card support for responder's minor (3♦) or if missing that too then perhaps she has a balanced minimum hand (3NT).

If responder had introduced a new suit, then opener's remaining alternatives are to show a stopper in the fourth suit (by bidding 3NT) or to bid the fourth suit itself to ask if responder has a stop there. In practice, responder might have already bid 3NT earlier with stops in all remaining suits and so opener's fourth suit bid in the third round of bidding after all three other suit had been bid will probably include a half-stop in the remaining fourth suit, not quite enough in itself for opener to be bidding 3NT.

If responder's second round of bidding was a low level fit-showing bid for opener's suit (1♠-2♣-2♠-3♠. i.e. slow) and therefore showing a good hand then a whole different set of prospects are in store for opener's third bid.

Opener would now only sign-off in game with a sub if not bare minimum hand (1♠-2♣-2♠-3♠-4♠). Responder had shown a good responder's hand but cue-bidding by opener on the way to game would still need more than a rock bottom minimum hand.

A possibility for a non-minimum opener. having received suit agreement, is to reciprocate with a fitting card in responder's suit (1♠-2♣-2♠-3♠-4♣). With enough extras and a proper fit she would have raised earlier. So this late raise does not necessarily show a double-fit now. Opener could be showing only a fitting honour (minimum Qx) and opener's suit remains agreed.

After receiving suit agreement. with most non-minimum hands our opener will more likely cue-bid a new suit (4♦ or 4♥) to show an ace and mild (non-serious) interest in slam. The cue-bid here does not promise much and is a courtesy cue-bid in case responder is interested in slam. When opener does have extras of her own and therefore is serious about slam prospects then her bid is 3NT ('serious 3NT') which asks responder to cue-bid whilst opener's declarer-hand remains undisclosed.

2.7   You've arrived

By the time opener has made her third round bid the 2-over-1 sequence will have usually provided enough information mutually for a sound decision as to the prospects with pushing beyond the game level. If you bid on, you will be well prepared for it.

But if you are signing off at game level you will no doubt be signing off also for the soundest of reasons that even the 5-level might be dangerous, which in the absence of these 2-over-1 methods others may well succumb to with a late slam investigation.

The third round of bidding is probably a good point to end our review of 2-over-1 methods. I hope the above tour of the system has convinced you of its merits and that you will choose to make it the central plank of your bidding system.

Let's not forget that even the absence of a 2-over-1 sequence, say instead a Forcing 1NT reply by responder on the first round, will often serve you well by keeping the bidding low and preventing you from going for unrealistic game attempts.

There is no damage done, either, if the occasion for the 2-over-1 methods does not arise at the table because, say, the opponents intervene with our opening bid. You will then be simply reverting to your usual standard methods.

But whenever the hands do embark on a 2-over-1 sequence you will be better off by the end of that sequence. Heads you win, tails you don't lose.

Chapter 3

Wide-Range 1NT Response to 1M

All variations of the 2-over-1 forcing-to-game system include the so-called Forcing No-Trump convention as an integral part of the system. It is used by responder to describe a wide range of hands that have less than game-forcing values.

Rather than a natural 1NT response to play, the Forcing 1NT response can have up to 11 HCP or even a bad-12. It also includes invitational hands with 3-card support for opener's major, which is another reason why opener will not pass it out. Hence it is 'forcing'. More specifically it is forcing for one round.

There is also the alternative of a Semi-Forcing No-Trump concept. In some versions of the 2-over-1 system this applies only to situations where responder is a passed hand, in other versions only where he is an unpassed hand, and in yet other versions it replaces the Forcing 1NT convention as a whole both for passed and unpassed hands.

The idea of the so-called semi-forcing no-trump is that opener should be free to pass the 1NT response if holding a minimum opening hand herself. So, opener is in effect allowed to convert the forcing 1NT bid to a natural 1NT to play by passing it out. Hence the 'semi-forcing' label, meaning that it does not necessarily oblige opener to make a second bid. Opener may pass with a balanced minimum hand given that responder's 1NT ruled out the prospects of game anyway.

I like the passable variety of the no-trump response, the so-called semi-forcing version, and I like it specifically when responder is an unpassed hand. This is the version adopted in this book's system.

Before I go on, a word on terminology. The rationale of the so-called 'semi-forcing' 1NT response is fine but I don't think the title sounds right. The idea of a responder's bid being a forcing bid if opener likes her own hand but non-forcing if she doesn't, appears to me as though it is simply a non-forcing bid as far as responder is concerned.

Equally importantly, I think that the opponent next to bid is entitled to a better classification of the 1NT response and whether or not the bidding is supposed to be coming round another time. Actually, I wouldn't be surprised if the rules in some bridge jurisdictions do not even allow optional half-way bid categories between forcing and non-forcing types.

Far from me to pick anyone on their use of the English language which after all is a second language for me, it nevertheless seems to me that the optional or contingent nature of the 1NT bid ought to be clear to the opponents at the point that the bid is made.

I personally like to refer to it as a "wide-ranging 6-11 HCP" response, and so avoid any 'forcing' label but instead actually spell out what it shows.

3.1 When the wide-range 1NT response applies

The first thing to say is that. for me. the wide range 6-11 HCP response only applies to an unpassed responder. When partner opens 1♥ or 1♠ and the next opponent passes, responder makes his natural raise or 1-level response if available. With other hands that are not strong enough to force to game. an unpassed responder can bid our wide-range 1NT showing:

- 6-11 HCP: and

- No 4-card spade suit in response to hearts; and

- No 4+card support for opener's major (covered by Bergen and direct raises): and

- No 3-card support for opener's major - except specifically in a 10-11 HCP hand

That exception is significant. It is a major strength of the system that invitational hands with 10-11 HCP and 3-card support start specifically with the 1NT response and then reveal precisely this hand type at the next opportunity as we will see shortly.

I do not favour it myself but the most commonly used versions of the Forcing 1NT response structure also include 5-7 HCP hands with 3-card support and 5-9 HCP hands with 2-card support, such that a direct raise of 1M-2M by an unpassed hand then becomes a constructive 3-card raise with 8-9 HCP. Some of this fine-tuning would be welcome but it does begin to mean that passing-out 1NT becomes less of an option even for a minimum-opener and that in any continuation opener never knows if responder's 2-level preference is on a 2-card suit or a 3-card suit and in practice final contracts on 5-2 major fits with mutually weak hands become frequent. On balance, I think it is better to retain the 1M-2M raise as a 6-9 HCP response but allow flexibility to a minimum opener to pass out a 1NT response.

3.2   Opener's second round options

In normal 2-over-1 methods opener can never pass responder's 1NT response if responder is an unpassed hand. As mentioned earlier, I favour a somewhat different approach here. The unpassed responder's 1NT is still 6-11 HCP for me but I like it that opener should be allowed to pass this out if she had opened with an undistinguished and fairly balanced 12-13 HCP hand.

In most versions of 2-over-1 the above flexibility is normally an option for opener only if responder was a passed hand and this passable 1NT is called a semi-forcing no-trump for that reason. Not for me.

I prefer it that, even facing 1NT by an unpassed responder, opener's first option is to pass out responder's 1NT response - if holding a 12-13 HCP balanced hand. Given that responder promised no more than 11 HCP, game is not a serious possibility when opener holds only 12-13 HCP. More to the point, with at least one of the hands balanced if not both, 1NT as a final contract is likely to play and score quite well - not an insignificant matter in matchpoints.

It is true that we are giving up the option of playing in 5-3 major-suit fits when the unpassed responder may be an invitational hand with 3-card fit. But any invitation would not have been taken up when opener is a minimum anyway and so we are not missing game. Indeed, a 5-3 fit will often take the same number of tricks in no-trumps to make it a matchpoints winner.

However, when blessed with more than a minimum balanced hand, opener must bid again to allow responder to complete the description of his hand. Opener's rebid here will show her strength and tell partner something new about her hand pattern. If she has extra length in her major or she holds a lower-ranking 4+ card side suit, she can now make a natural, descriptive rebid. But with some other types of hands, she may have to bid a 3-card minor as a last resort. Here are opener's other rebid options:

12-13 HCP unbalanced hands and all 14-15 HCP hands:

- Rebid the major if holding 6+ cards in the suit

- Bid 2♥ if you had opened 1♠ and also hold 4+ cards in hearts

- Bid 2 of the longer minor with all other hands, promising only 3+ cards in the suit

- With a precise 4-5-2-2 hand pattern (four spades) opener has to rebid 2♥

16 to a poor-18 HCP:

- Rebid 3 of the major if it is a good 6+ card suit (invitational)

- Raise to 2NT with balanced 18 HCP or 4-5-2-2 hands with a very good 16 to a mediocre 17 count (invitational)

- Reverse to 2♠ with 17+ HCP with 4-5 in the majors (forcing)

- Bid 2 of the longer minor with all other hands up to 17 HCP (not forcing)

Good-18 or more HCP:

- Jump-raise to 3NT with a semi-balanced 19+ HCP or a very strong 18 HCP

- Reverse to 2♠ if you were 4-5 in the majors (forcing)

- Make a jump-shift (high-reverse) to 3 of a lower-ranking 4+ card suit (forcing)

Opener's values are placed within a very narrow range when she rebids her major or raises no-trumps. On the other hand, if her second round bid is in a lower-ranking new suit she can have a significantly wider range. After 1♠-1NT, a rebid of 2♣, 2♦ or 2♥ could be made with as many as 17 HCP. Responder can pass these rebids but if he has 9+ HCP he must bid again to keep the auction live. Only this way will opener be able to reveal her extra strength which she could not bring out in her second bid.

Some hands require good judgment on the part of opener with her second round bid. She can upgrade her hand with good suits or distribution but otherwise she should keep to the script.

For example, 6-4 hands need particularly good judgment. Over partner's 1NT response, should you show the extra length in your first suit or bring your second suit into the auction? There can be no clear-cut answer but some general considerations could be as follows. If you are a minimum then it is often best to rebid your first suit and limit your hand, unless the relative suit quality allows you to rebid hearts to bring out your second major after you opened spades.

Strong 6-4 hands are easier to bid because you can reverse into a higher ranking 4-card second suit or jump-shift into a lower ranking one. But if you have intermediate values in the 15-17 HCP range, then it is probably best to introduce your second suit by a simple rebid, hoping that partner can bid again. If he does, you will be in a very good position because now you can invite game and partner will also be aware that you have some extras for not having simply rebid your first suit.

3.3 Responder's second bid

After opener's rebid, it is time for responder to clarify his strength and the basis of his original 1NT response. Was it a search for the best part-score contract or did he have an invitational hand?

With a weak hand in 6-9 HCP range and evidently no fit for opener's original major:

- Pass opener's second suit (minimum 4-card fit for a minor, 3-card fit for hearts)

- Give false-preference to opener's original major (with a doubleton)

- Sign-off in a non-jump new suit (6+ cards at 3-level; strong 5+ cards at 2-level)

- Accept opener's game invitations when holding 8-9 HCP

With an invitational hand in 10-11 HCP range:

- Bid 2NT denying fit for partner's major and showing stoppers in unbid suits

- Jump to 3-level in partner's major with 3-card support (1♥-1NT-2♣-3♥)

- Raise partner's major rebid (1♠-1NT-2♠-3♠ needs 2 cards but 1♥-1NT-2♥-3♥ should have 3-card support)

- Raise partner's second major with 4-card fit (1♠-1NT-2♥-3♥)

- Raise partner's minor rebid with weak/fair 5+ card support (1♥-1NT-2♣-3♣)

- Bid an 'impossible 2♠' as a good raise for partner's minor suit rebid after opening in hearts (1♥-1NT-2♣-2♠)

- Jump in a previously unbiddable strong 6+ card heart suit (1♠-1NT-2♣-3♥)

- Bid 3NT or 4M with a maximum hand which improved further after opener's rebid.

Responder's 2♠ rebid in the sequence 1♥-1NT-2♣-2♠ cannot be a spade-suit because he would have shown that over 1♥.

3.4 When the wide-range 1NT response does not apply

The wide-range 1NT response applies only after partner opens a major. 1♥ or 1♠. It does not apply when partner opens a minor. 1♦ or 1♣. In the sequences 1♦-1NT and 1♣-1NT (or 1♣-1♠* if playing transfer responses to 1♣). responder's 1NT is the usual 6-10 HCP with a minor suit flavour and non-forcing.

The wide-range 1NT idea also does not apply when the first opponent overcalls. After an intervening overcall the 1NT response reverts to its non-forcing meaning of 6-10 HCP with stopper(s) in the opponent's suit.

If the first opponent doubles partner's 1♥ or 1♠ opening bid. the wide-range 1NT again is disbanded; responder reverts to normal partnership methods (which in the system in this book would be transfer responses).

Of course all the above are for an unpassed responder in the first place.

3.5 Passed hand responder

In so far as a passed hand responder is concerned. unlike in most versions of the 2-over-1 system I do not like the idea of ascribing either a forcing or a semi-forcing attribute to anything he may bid. Given that as a passed hand he cannot force to game, opener should be allowed to pass any response.

Indeed there is no reason for the passed hand responder's 1NT to be wide range any more. I think it is much clearer systematically to play a passed hand responder's 1NT as a perfectly natural 6-9 HCP bid, or even a bad or awkward 10 HCP, but in any event not forward-going.

A 1NT response by a passed hand also always denies support for partner's major. If you have 3-card or better support, with 6-9 HCP it is best to raise opener directly to the level of the fit (so, 2M, 3M or 4M) and with 10-11 HCP we have another tool to use - Drury, to which I turn next.

3.6   Drury

The Drury Convention is an artificial 2♣ response by a passed hand after partner opens 1♥ or 1♠ in third or fourth seat. It shows an invitational hand with 3 cards or better trump support and maximum playing values, 10-11 HCP including distributional upgrade.

The distributional feature could be a ruffing potential given the fit or a good side-suit. The pure HCP count could be as low as 8-9 HCP in some cases.

Drury brings out strong feelings among bridge players; some love it, others hate it. Those who are against it regard the entire enterprise at best as an unnecessary sacrifice of a perfectly useful natural bid and at worst as a misadventure to control semi-physic weak opening bids.

On the other hand, those who are for Drury see it as a valuable convention that comes up frequently. is easy to remember and an improvement to bidding accuracy which solves an insurmountable issue about invitational passed hands with support for opener's major.

Indeed, in the absence of an artificial tool such as Drury. responder cannot possibly always get it right. He might raise to the 3-level and go down because opener was light; he may underbid to only the 2-level and make two overtricks when opener was full-value; he might try 1NT but opener may pass that when the 8-card fit would have played better, etc.

A Drury 2♣ response eliminates the prospect of such disasters by allowing you to show your support and strength in one bid without getting too high. It also provides a let-out if partner had indeed opened light but ensures continued bidding when she was full value.

In fact. with Drury in your arsenal. the partnership understanding for opening with 1♥ or 1♠ in third or fourth seat can be safely anchored to the Rule of 19. rather than Rule of 20. counting the number of cards in your two longest suits plus all your high card points.

In reply to 2♣ opener's rebid clarifies her hand. There are different ways of doing this. The following scheme. modelled mostly on Reverse Drury but with some tweaks of my own. uses opener's rebid of her original major to announce a poor hand whereas all other bids are natural and show at least a full opener. The rebids are:

- 2M rebid is bare minimum (11-12 HCP)

- 2♦ is artificial and shows sound opening bid (13-14 HCP) but no particular extras

- 2♥ (after 1♠-2♣) shows sound opening bid (13-14 HCP) with 4-card side heart suit

- Rebids higher than 2M show extra values and/or shape and are invitational

- 2NT is 14 HCP balanced

- 3NT is 18-19 HCP balanced

Drury complements our passed hand responder's options alongside a natural 1NT response whereas our unpassed responder has got the wide range 1NT response as the main tool for all less than game force hands.

Chapter 4

Transfer Responses to 1♣

4.1   The rationale

A distinct advantage of transfer responses is that the transfer-request by responder allows an opportunity for opener to give an additional message in her rebid by accepting or breaking the transfer and at the same time responder gains an extra bid to give another message on his part when opener's rebid comes back to him.

This idea can be applied to many other bidding situations. Indeed the idea of transfer responses after partner opens 1NT has been the norm in bridge for a very long time. There are other situations where it also works well, such as after partner is doubled or when partner overcalls. Applying the same idea to 1♣ openings is very sensible because some of the time it is not an honest club suit anyway and, for the sacrifice of one single natural response (1♦), it enables an array of additional sequences and fine-tuning in bidding.

Transfer responses to a 1♣ opening bid are not unusual any more. But the particulars of the response methodology here in this book may well be a surprise to some readers.

Most transfer response schemes generically speaking, and in fact all other transfer schemes to 1♣ that I have personally come across, build on the idea of accepting the transfer to indicate a liking of the target suit, usually a minimum of 3 cards in the suit. But, it seems to me that, if the opponents are not overcalling then it works considerably better if this approach is reversed - that opener completes the transfer to show her dislike.

So, the structure I propose here, and what I have actually been playing for many years to good effect, is based on the premise of completing a transfer with weak hands and no fit for the transfer suit. In other words, completion of the transfer is an early warning to partner that things do not look good.

Breaking the transfer, on the other hand, is good news. In our system here, breaking the transfer promises either a weak hand with tolerance for responder's suit (2-3 cards) or a good hand in which case a fit with responder's suit will not be critical anyway.

4.2   The transfer structure

When opener opens 1♣ and the first opponent passes or doubles, responder's first bid up to and including the 2NT bid is a transfer to the next suit or no-trumps denomination up the line:

1♣*-(p/x)-1♦*	Shows 4+ hearts, 6+ HCP, (natural 1♦ not available)
1♣*-(p/x)-1♥*	Shows 4+ spades, 6+ HCP
1♣*-(p/x)-1♠*	6-10 or 16+ HCP, balanced, with ♣/♦, no majors
1♣*-(p/x)-1N*	10+ HCP inverted-raise to 2♣, 5+ clubs
1♣*-(p/x)-2♣*/♦*/♥*	3-way transfers to next strain (see page 57)
1♣*-(p/x)-2♠*	11-12 HCP balanced, denies 4+ card major
1♣*-(p/x)-2N*	8-9 HCP inverted-raise to 3♣, 5+ clubs
1♣*-(p/x)-3♣*	6-7 HCP inverted-raise to 3♣, 5+ clubs

The above transfer responses apply only if the first opponent passes or doubles. They do not apply if the first opponent overcalls opener's 1♣ bid with a suit overcall or a no-trumps overcall, in which case responder reverts to our normal and natural responses.

The 1♣ opening bid should of course be announced in the first place as one that could be a 2-card suit and all the transfer responses need to be alerted.

This initial relay by responder gains additional bidding space with many alternative sequences now becoming available. If the second opponent intervenes, even more sequences are gained.

This added flexibility also takes some pressure off the wide-ranging 1♣ opening bid and often lets opener complete defining her hand quite specifically before opponents get in at all.

Above all the system helps us to identify misfits sooner and bail out or pass accordingly.

4.3   If the second opponent passes

If the second opponent passes, opener will simply complete the transfer to show a 12-14 HCP hand type with no fit (only 0-1 card in case of a transfer to a major or 2 cards in case of clubs). So, completing the transfer in the simplest way is a warning and shows lack of interest. As responder could still have a big hand, opener is merely keeping the bidding open:

1♣*-(p/x)-1♦*-(p)-1♥*	Simple completion, 12-14 HCP, 0-1 hearts only
1♣*-(p/x)-1♥*-(p)-1♠*	Simple completion, 12-14 HCP, 0-1 spades only
1♣*-(p/x)-1N*-(p)-2♣*	Inverted raise obliged, 12-14 HCP, 2 clubs only

Simple completion as above is alertable because it specifically denies interest.

With most weak hands (12-14 HCP) communicating the lack of fit with responder's suit by completing the transfer is a priority for opener's rebid over and above introducing a new 4-card suit. This is not as dangerous as it sounds because responder will rarely pass out the completion when he is so expressly told that he can expect no support.

If for example opener completes the transfer and responder only had a 4 or even 5-card suit then it is incumbent upon him to scramble to the 'best' final contract, perhaps 1NT.

But more often our opener will bypass the transfer suit and make her natural rebid, this constructive rebid now implying EITHER at least a 2-card tolerance for responder's major if weak (12-14) OR usually any 15+ HCP hand which is therefore not particularly concerned about fit with responder.

If opener bypasses the transfer and rebids 1NT then this is always a balanced 12-14 HCP hand anyway but in this system it positively means 2 or 3 card fit for responder's major (but not a 4 card fit, with which opener would have jump-completed the transfer).

Even if opener bypasses the transfer to simply rebid a second suit (a higher ranking suit at 1-level or a lower ranking suit at the 2-level) then the implication is still that she holds 2 or 3 cards (more often 2) in responder's suit if she only had 12-14 HCP for her opening. That's because with only 0-1 card in responder's major and a weak hand she would have completed the transfer as a warning - rather than introduce a second suit.

The 2-3 card 'fit' implied in opener's breaking of the transfer, even when weak, should also be able to withstand responder's possible weak 5-6 card sign-off rebid in that suit at 2-level. So, the best contract is probably still reached when mutually weak.

But, if holding 15+ HCP then, irrespective of fit, opener always resumes the normal (forcing or non-forcing) rebid that the hand would have made ignoring the transfer. A jump rebid in NT without opponents intervening would show the 18-19 HCP balanced hand type (or a non-jump 2NT rebid if opponents intervened at 2-level); and any other suit rebid bypassing the transfer suit now unravels an unbalanced hand type.

A potentially problematic holding for opener is a weak but unbalanced hand with long(er) clubs. When she opens 1♣ and hears partner transfer into her shortage, she needs to decide whether to treat it as primarily a weak hand (and complete the transfer) or mislead partner for at least a 2-card fit (and ignore/break the transfer). Playing an intermediate 6-card club suit as a 3♣ opener avoids some of this potential problem.

But breaking the transfer is almost always a constructive and favourable development (although if a non-forcing or a limit rebid, it can still be passed). Typical sequences, with the second opponent still passing after the first opponent had passed or doubled, are:

1♣*-(p/x)-1♦*-(p)-1♠	Normal rebid, 4234 or 4324 or 4225 shape, etc
1♣*-(p/x)-1♦*-(p)-1N	Normal rebid, 12-14 HCP with 2-3 hearts
1♣*-(p/x)-1♦*-(p)-2♣	Normal rebid, unbalanced, 5+ clubs, 12+ HCP
1♣*-(p/x)-1♦*-(p)-2♦	Normal rebid, reverse-bid, forcing, etc
1♣*-(p/x)-1♦*-(p)-2♥	Normal rebid ('jump'), 12-14 HCP with 4 hearts
1♣*-(p/x)-1♦*-(p)-2♠	Normal rebid, reverse-bid, forcing, etc
1♣*-(p/x)-1♥*-(p)-3♦	Normal rebid, splinter, spades-agreed
1♣*-(p/x)-1♠*-(p)-2N	Normal rebid, 18-19 HCP
1♣*-(p/x)-1N*-(p)-2♦	Normal rebid, ♦-stopper as NT-probe, 12+ HCP

I did not mark any opener's rebid with an asterisk to suggest that it should necessarily be alerted because the rebid is perfectly natural as it stands and one that would be made with or without a transfer response. My other reason is that the alert explanation if one was to be made is quite cumbersome to spell out. But if you are concerned that your bridge jurisdiction may treat the transfer break as passing particularly valuable additional information then it would be best to alert it and provide an explanation.

The proper alert explanation for opener's rebid breaking the transfer in the first two examples above would be to say that it shows "EITHER 2-3 card support in a 12-14 HCP hand; OR any hand usually unconcerned with fit for responder on account of its own shape or strength". In other cases there may be a specific explanation available: specifically 4-card support in example 5; reverse in examples 4 and 6; splinter in example 7, etc.

So, if the second opponent passes, our side will always be reverting to normal bidding with opener's rebid unless she is both weak and has less than 2-card support. (It is possible to build more relay sequences here but that is for another day).

The most common sequence is the example 2 above; responder transfers to a major and opener rebids 1NT ('weak-NT'). After this start, with a forward-going hand responder may now invoke a New Minor Forcing (or some other checkback) sequence, or, if responder passes then the hand gets to be played by opener (the same side as weak-NT openers).

4.4   If the second opponent doubles 1♥* (transfer to spades)

If responder's transfer request is doubled by the second opponent, it may well be unclear what this opponent is trying to say to his/her partner. There is probably not much point in asking in case unauthorised information may flow especially in the absence of screens. Instead our side should take their double at face value and assume that it was naturally trying to show a liking for the cipher suit.

For opener to volunteer a bid or completion after the double she should have reason: she should have either extra values or minimum 3-card support or both. A 5-card club suit could also be a reason to get in a club rebid and clarify the opening bid.

If strong. opener will not be concerned about missing a fit and can afford to show her hand's non-minimum values first by breaking the transfer and resuming a normal rebid. as before. So. after 1♣*-(p)-1♥*-(x). a strong opener's options are:

XX	Support redouble with 3 spades and 15+ HCP
1N	15+ (not 12-14 after double). ♥-stop. maybe 1-3-4-5 shape
2♦	Reverse. forcing
2♥	15+ cue bid of 'opponent's suit'. multi-purpose force
2N	18-19 HCP after opponent's double with ♥-stopper(s)

But if opener has the 12-14 HCP hand type then the priority with her rebid is to clarify her holding in responder's transfer target suit by passing. completing. or raising. Thus. after 1♣*-(p)-1♥*-(x). a weak opener's options are:

P	12-14 HCP. 0-2 cards in partner's spades
1♠	3-card spade suit but with 12-14 HCP (redouble with 15+)
2♣	Natural. 5+ clubs. not 3 spades. could still be 12 HCP
2♠	12-14 HCP 'jump' raise with 4-card spade fit

Please note that we have both a redouble and 1♠-completion to show 3-card spade fit and so we can differentiate our strength; redouble with 15+ HCP but just complete the transfer with only 12-14 HCP.

After the second opponent doubles, the guiding principle for the opener is to make a 'voluntary' completion/redouble of the transfer only if holding 3-card support (rather like the situation when we would have 'voluntarily' completed a transfer following a 1NT opening, a transfer by partner and an intervention by the second opponent ahead of opener's rebid).

So the complete range of opener rebids after responder transfers to spades and the second opponent doubles are as follows, starting with 1♣*-(p)-1♥*-(x):

P	No voluntary bid or completion, 12-14 HCP, 0-2 spades
XX	Support redouble with 3 spades, 15+ HCP
1♠	Voluntary completion, 3-cards (again) but here 12-14 HCP
1N	15+ HCP voluntary bid; ♥-stopper(s), maybe 1-3-4-5 shape
2♣	Natural, 5+ clubs, 12+ HCP, not 3 spades
2♦	Reverse, forcing
2♥	15+ HCP cue of 'opponent's suit', multi-purpose force
2♠	12-14 HCP with 4 spades, a 'jump' raise
2N	18-19 HCP after opponent's double with ♥-stopper(s)

4.5   If the second opponent doubles 1♦* (transfer to hearts)

Equally common is the situation where responder bids diamonds as transfer to hearts and the second opponent doubles. Here we can generally use the same structure but redouble in this case should not solely be a support redouble whilst the other major remains unclaimed by either side. I suggest that redouble here should be a 'negative-redouble' showing 4 spades as well as 3 hearts. This works because we also have a 1♠ rebid available to show 4 spades without 3 hearts (and opener cannot have more than 4 spades after having opened 1♣ unless she had a 6-5 clubs-spades combination).

So, the complete range of opener rebids after responder transfers to hearts and the second opponent doubles, 1♣*-(p)-1♦*-(x), would be as follows:

P	No voluntary bid or completion, 12-14 HCP, 0-2 hearts
XX	Negative redouble, 4 spades and 3 hearts
1♥	Voluntary completion, 3 hearts, 12-14 (15) HCP
1♠	4+ card spade suit (again) but here denying 3 hearts
1N	15+ HCP voluntary bid, ♦-stopper(s), maybe 3-1-4-5 shape
2♣	Natural, 5+ clubs, 12+ HCP, not 3 hearts, not 4 spades
2♦	15+ HCP cue of 'opponent's suit', multi-purpose force
2♥	12-14 HCP with 4 hearts, a 'jump' raise
2♠	Reverse, forcing
2N	18-19 HCP after opponent's double, ♦-stopper(s)

One of the overall points of above structure following partner's transfer and opponent's intervention is that opener makes voluntary rebids only with a reason. If she is strong then she can ignore the double. But if she is weak she can only bid on because she has either a natural 5-card club rebid. or at least 3-card support for partner's major. or a claim to the other major.

Non-descript 12-14 HCP hands even with a stopper in the suit implied by opponent's double must pass as a rule - and hope that partner can reopen with a redouble in which case opener can choose between a pass and 1NT for her third round call.

The inference is that if opener's second bid was a pass this in fact summarily clarifies the hand as a minimum in more ways than one - weak BOTH in points AND in support for partner's major - so that responder can judge the subsequent developments well and act/refrain accordingly.

4.6   If the second opponent intervenes in a suit

If the second opponent intervenes in a suit. opener can generally resume normal rebidding without any inconvenience to our side. In fact the inconvenience is usually all theirs.

When responder makes a transfer by bidding the suit below that he holds, the next opponent holding the bid suit is usually compromised between making a natural double or bidding that suit at 2-level. If their double is natural then they lose their negative double option unless they have an agreement to instead bid our transfer suit as takeout. Only their 5+ card overcalls in the remaining two suits retain their usual meaning.

Our opener, on the other hand, retains all her options over the second opponent's intervention. A double would be a takeout double showing the other major if available but a support-double for partner's major if the opponent's intervention claimed the other major. So. after for example 1♣*-(p)-1♦*-(1♠), opener rebids as follows:

P	No voluntary bid or completion, 12-14 HCP, 0-2 hearts
X	Support double with 3 hearts, 12+ HCP, unlimited
1N	15+ HCP (not 12-14) with ♠-stopper(s), not 3 hearts
2♣	Natural, 5+ clubs, 12+ HCP, not 3 hearts
2♦	Reverse, forcing
2♥	12-14 HCP with 4 hearts, a 'jump' raise
2♠	15+ HCP cue bid of opponent's suit, multi-purpose force
2N	18-19 HCP after opponent's double with ♠-stopper(s)

Incidentally, I like to use the 2♠ cue bid here (and most of my cue bids) as a general-purpose force rather than more specifically as an Unassuming Cue Bid or Directional Asking Bid or Western Cue Bid. But partner has to have an order of priority in replying to the cue bid and I like the order that partner should take it, firstly, as asking for a stopper in the cue-suit for no-trumps purposes (and respond on that basis) but remain open to the idea that it may yet turn out. secondly. to be a sound raise of partner's suit, and, thirdly, some other general purpose force which you will clarify later (such as having your own agenda perhaps based on a good suit of your own).

4.7 If either opponent intervenes with 1NT

As usual, a double by us of either opponent's intervening no-trumps overcall is for penalties: -

1♣*-(1N)-x	Penalty double
1♣*-(p)-1♥*-(1N)-x	Penalty double
1♣*-(x)-1♥*-(1N)-x	Penalty double

The doubler expects partner to pass the penalty but is prepared for partner to take it out if very weak and so must have tolerance (at least a doubleton) for any suit partner had shown previously.

4.8 Responder's rebid

The bidding may well proceed to a second-round bid by responder without any intervention.

If opener's rebid showed a minimum and no fit, responder decides the best final contract. So, after 1♣*-(p)-1♦*-(p)-1♥*-(p), responder settles as follows:

P	Weak with 6 hearts or 5 good ones and nowhere else to go
1♠	4 spades, 4+ hearts, non-forcing
1N	4+ hearts, semi-balanced, to play
2♣	Hearts and (maybe longer) clubs, non-forcing
2♦	Hearts and (maybe longer) diamonds, to play
2♥	6-7 semi-solid hearts, invitational
2♠	4+ spades, 5+ hearts, forcing to 3♥
2N	11-12 HCP, fairly balanced, only 5 hearts
3♣	Natural and forcing
3♦	Natural and forcing
3♥	Natural and forcing with 7+ hearts
3♠	5 spades, 5+hearts, forcing to game
3N	To play

But we could just as easily deal with a protective double by the first opponent. So, after 1♣*-(p)-1♦*-(p)-1♥*-(x), responder clarifies his position:

P	Weak with 6 hearts or 5 good ones, prepared to play
2♥	Reassuring opener, 6-7 hearts, happy to play
XX	SOS - responder had only 4 hearts!
Other	Other bids as before as if no double

Or, if there is a protective double by the second opponent, 1♣*-(p)-1♦*-(p)-1♥*-(p)-p-(x), then this time opener clarifies the basis of her original completion of the transfer:

P	Opener has singleton heart
XX	SOS - void in hearts
1N	To play
Other	Good 5 card suit to play (and 0-1 hearts)

Responder's rebids will be entirely natural if opener's rebid had bypassed the transfer request in the first place and already returned the auction to natural bidding.

4.9   3-way jump-transfer responses to 1♣

Transfer responses to a 1♣ opening bid lend themselves to many other ideas. Take the jump responses at 2-level. If we were playing weak-jump responses before then we can still play them. In fact the relay nature of responder's first bid now make it possible to assign two alternative options to the jump-transfer-response. When the completion of the transfer comes back to him, he can pass it as one option or he can go on to make another bid as an alternative option. So a 2-way transfer jump-shift.

Never mind 2-way. how about a 3-way jump-shift? Assuming the first opponent has passed or doubled the 1♣ opening bid. so the transfer sytem is on. here is a specific 3-way transfer jump-shift scheme.   starting   with   a   sequence   such   as 1♣*-(p/x)-2♦*-(p)-2♥-(p/x) and with responder to speak again:

Option 1: Pass out 2♥	Initial 2♦* was a responder's weak-2 in hearts
Option 2: Raise hearts (3♥)	2♦* was a single-suited game force in hearts
Option 3: Raise clubs (3♣)	2♦* was a jump-fit in clubs and hearts!

When faced with a jump-transfer opener initially assumes responder to have a weak-2 type hand and so simply completes the transfer on all hand types with which he may have passed a weak-2 opening bid from partner. The threshold to break the transfer (which could include a 2NT Ogust-type enquiry, or any other natural/forcing bid) should be set much higher (16+ HCP or 6-losers) facing jump-transfers as compared to 1-level transfers. We will discuss weak jumps shifts more specifically, including the Ogust enquiry, on pages 71 to 73 in Minor Suit Sequences.

The 3-way jump-transfers can be played in 3 suits, as follows:

1♣*-(p/x)- 2♣*	3-way transfer to diamonds
1♣*-(p/x)- 2♦*	3-way transfer to hearts
1♣*-(p/x)- 2♥*	3-way transfer to spades

4.10   Defence to opponents playing similar transfer responses to 1♣

If the opponents are playing transfer responses themselves then we will first know about it in the fourth seat, over the responding-opponent's transfer bid. Rather than present a disadvantage, this may in fact provide us with a choice of alternative overcalls. A double can show the artificially-bid suit and we can bid the transfer suit itself as a takeout of that suit (with 4 cards in the other major). So. after (1♣*)-p-(1♦*):

X   12+ HCP with diamonds;

1♥*   Takeout double of hearts, with 4 spades;

1♠   5+ spades, 12+ HCP

We can keep to this 4th seat defence even if we doubled (rather than pass) in the 2nd seat.

4.11   Summary

When we open 1♣ and the first opponent passes or doubles. responder's first bid up to and including 2NT is a transfer to the next suit or no-trumps denomination up the line.

We no longer have a natural 1♦ response available and so our 1♠ response (transfer to 1NT) may now have a diamond flavour just as much as a club flavour.

The transfer response enables opener a further opportunity to re-define her hand not only in terms of her points range but often also in terms of her fit with partner's suit.

Opener rebids simply with a minimum hand and no immediate fit (0-1 card major-suit 'fit') or pass if the second opponent intervenes.

Unlike most other transfer/relay systems, the idea of completing the transfer with weak-and-misfit hands as in this system in this book is unusual. Our system does not have a name (though it would be nice if it were to stick and become known as Kaban transfers!)

In order to break the transfer and resume a normal rebid instead, opener needs to have either at least a 2 card tolerance for partner or any 15+ HCP hand for which a fit with partner's suit is not an issue. On a good day opener may even have both tolerance for partner's suit and a good hand of her own.

When breaking the transfer and reverting to a normal rebid, opener recalls what her hand would have rebid if we had not been playing transfer responses to 1♣ openings and partner had replied naturally, and, most of the time, she now simply makes that same normal rebid. The difference is that the fact and the nature of any intervention by the second opponent over responder's transfer request will now also allow opener many additional sequences to fine-tune her rebid with more specific messages.

Opener's rebid may even include such tools as a 'takeout-redouble', which kind-of follows and builds on our other gem of a dual use for a double/redouble as 'negative' if the other major is still available but as 3-card support for partner's major if the other major had been bid/claimed.

For avoidance of doubt, in case the situation gets complicated in later bidding, our subsequent cue-bids etc, always treat our responder's transfer request as if it was a bid made in the underlying anchor suit in the first place. Conversely we always treat the opponents' attack on our artificial transfer bid as if they mean to show interest in that artificial cipher suit.

This system is open to many additional ideas and relay sequences. Currently, as a specific additional feature, I have suggested turning certain jump-transfers into 3-way relays. I hope to follow up with more transfer ideas at a later date, starting perhaps with the introduction of transfer sequences also after the first opponent overcalls.

Chapter 5

Minor Suit Sequences

5.1 1♣ opening bid on a 2+ card suit

I am a strong advocate of using the 1♣ opening bid as promising a minimum of only 2 cards in the suit, not 3. I think that this style has a lot going for it especially when playing transfer responses to a 1♣ opening, which was discussed in Chapter 4.

In any event the only hand pattern which would make an opening bid of 1♣ necessary on a 2-card club suit is the precise 4-4-3-2 shape. The rest of the time there will be at least a 3-card suit when we open 1♣.

With 3-3 in the minors I favour opening 1♣, not only to provide a bit more room for our bidding, but also so that this generates a transfer response sequence.

If the 1♣ opening bid actually included a proper club suit, then it is useful to play that opener's rebid in a major becomes a dual-purpose bid confirming a club suit alongside the major. So, for example 1♣-1♦*-1♠ confirms that opener has clubs and spades (which could be 4-4) and clears up any unambiguity about the original club bid. It follows that, holding a genuine club suit, it is important never to supress a major in one's rebid even if the hand is generally balanced in the 12-14 HCP range.

The corollary to the above principle is that when opener rebids 1NT or 2NT this does not deny a major; it only denies a major-club combination. So, without a club suit alongside the major, opener must now bypass the major suit and instead rebid in no-trumps with all balanced hands.

Of course any bypassed major suit will not remain buried forever. A New Minor Forcing enquiry (or any other form of checkback) by responder will still locate any major suit fit when he has a forward-going hand.

5.2 1♦ opening bid on a 4+ card suit

This system's 1♦ opening bid, on the other hand, always promises at least a 4-card diamond suit.

This contrast with the 1♣ is both useful and important. For one thing, the 1♦ opener is no longer potentially-short or ambiguous any more and so partner can rely on it.

In addition, this fact of a proper diamond suit in the first place also means that opener's rebid does not need to be dual-purpose anymore. In other words, there is no urgency for opener to rebid 1♠ over partner's 1♥ response. Indeed, she only needs to rebid 1♠ when the hand is particularly unbalanced - either with at least 5-diamonds alongside 4-spades or with a precise 4-1-4-4 shape. The shape requirement for a spade rebid is more specifically distributional after 1♦ than it was after 1♣.

The corollary this time is that, after a 1♦-1♥ start, opener will rebid 1NT supressing a spade-suit with all other balanced hands even including 4-4 in spades and diamonds. But again this does not mean that the 4-card spade suit will be lost. A New Minor Forcing enquiry (or some other checkback) by responder will still locate any suppressed major suit fit when he has the appropriate hand to continue bidding.

5.3   Inverted raise with a difference

Once upon a time the style of raising the minor suits was rather like the principles governing the raise of major suits. The sequence 1 minor-2 minor was weak and the sequence 1 minor-3 minor was stronger.

Then came the revolutionary idea in the Kaplan-Sheinwold system to simply reverse, or invert, those meanings. Since then it has become commonplace over the years to play 1m-2m as the stronger raise, so much so that there is now probably a couple of generations of bridge players who have never even heard of the previous methods and are possibly wondering which invertion the name refers to.

The switch makes a lot of sense. When responder is weak with a fit for opener's minor he wants to pre-empt and raise the level at which the opponents have to negotiate their intervention. This applies even more so if the first opponent doubles our 1m opening bid.

Conversely, when responder is strong he wants to communicate his fit at the lowest level possible and leave more room to explore the hands. This too makes a lot of sense.

When the first opponent, on the other hand, overcalls, rather than pass or double, it has been the received wisdom that our responder shows a good raise in opener's minor by making a cue bid (unassuming cue bid) of the opponent's overcall suit. But, I do not think that this is the best use of the bidding space.

It is true that the cue bid takes away a level of bidding from the second opponent and stops a simple raise of the first opponent's overcall. But competitive bidding methods can easily deal with such bids and, for example, a double by the advancer can show support for the overcall. More to the point, however, our responder's cue bid equally takes away a level of bidding from us and that is the main reason for my objections to the admittedly universal use of the unassuming cue bid here.

I would have thought that responder would have even more reason to go slowly when he has a fit and the values to compete. Surely the sequence 1♦-(1♠)-2♦ leaves more room for our side to explore our further options than the sequence 1♦-(1♠)-2♠*.

Realistically, when we have a fit in a minor and they in a major, they will have methods to outbid us when they must. Our main target here would be to investigate 3NT possibilities rather than 5 in the minor. If so, I think we want more room to investigate, not less.

It is for these reasons that I favour playing inverted minor suit raises, not just when opponents pass or double, but even after they overcall. I have been playing it this way to good effect for as long as I can remember.

So, with or without intervention, I suggest the following in the case of diamonds:

1♦- 2♦			10+ HCP and 4+card raise, also applies after intervention
→	→	2♥	Opener has heart-stop (but does not deny spade-stop), 12+
→	→	2♥- 2♠	Opener has heart-stop, responder confirms spade-stop
→	→	2♥- 2N	Opener has heart-stop, responder has probable spade-stop
→	→	2♠	Opener has spade-stop and denies heart-stop
→	→	2NT	Opener has exact 14 HCP
→	→	3♦	5+ diamonds, not forward-going
→	→	3NT	18-19 HCP
→	2NT		11-12 HCP balanced, probably no 4-card major
→	3♣		8-9 HCP and 4+card ♦-raise, also applies after intervention
→	3♦		6-7 HCP and 4+card raise, also applies after intervention
→	3♥/3♠/4♣		12-15 HCP, splinter raise in diamonds, denies a 4 card major

With clubs it is a little trickier because we also need to allow for transfer responses (if the first opponent is passing or doubling) as well as allowing for a natural raise (if he is overcalling). So, bearing

in mind that our transfer responses to 1♣ are off when the first
opponent overcalls. here is how responder raises clubs depending on
the first opponent's actions:

1♣-(1♥)-2♣	Inverted ♣-raise, 5+cards, 10+HCP: still inverted after overcall
1♣-(p/x)-1N*	Transfer ♣-raise, 5+cards, 10+HCP: transfer-raise if no overcall

Thereafter the continuations are much the same whether or not
there has been an overcall, except that the first sequence below is
specific to the no-overcall situation and some common-sense change
is appropriate with the 2NT and 3♣ responses if there was an
overcall:

1♣-1N*-2♣		Simple completion showing only 2-card club suit, 12-14 HCP
→	→ 2other	3+ clubs, stop in suit shown, no stop if bypassed, 12+ HCP
→	→ 2N	Opener has exact 14 HCP, 3+ clubs
→	→ 3♣	5+ clubs, not forward-going
→	→ 3N	18-19 HCP
→	2N*	8-9 HCP, 5+cards ♣-raise (but natural 11 HCP after overcall)
→	3♣	6-7 HCP, 5+cards raise (but 6-9 HCP raise after overcall)
→	3♦/♥/♠	12-15 HCP, splinter raise in clubs, denies a 4 card Major

There are ways to deal with an intervention by the second opponent
too:

1♦-(p)- 2♦-(2M)-p	Opener's pass shows weak-NT hand
→ → → → → (p)-x	Responder's double reconvenes our sequence

Some raises apply equally to diamonds and clubs:

1m-3N   Natural, 12-15 HCP, to play, minor-suit flavour, denying majors

1m-4m   Minor-suit RKCB (see page 162)

If the inverted raise to 2m is still available even after opponents' overcall, then this frees a cue-bid of the opponents' suit to become more of a stopper-seeking cue-bid as I also suggest elsewhere, such as on page 54. To recap, I like the cue-bid to be more flexible and that partner should take it primarily as asking for a stopper in the cue-suit for no-trumps purposes (and respond on that basis) but remain open to the idea that it may yet turn out to be a sound raise of partner's suit or maybe even some other general-purpose force which you will clarify later (such as having your own agenda perhaps based on a good suit of your own). This style seems a lot more user-friendly to me.

5.4   Impossible major as good raise of minor

After a sequence such as 1♣-1♠*-2♦, where your 1♠* showed a 1NT-response (in effect denying majors) and partner reversed into 2♦, your priority is to show your preference between partner's minors. Wouldn't it be also nice to be able to actually indicate your enthusiasm for one of those minors rather than an enforced false preference?

Well, you can have it all. Having already denied both majors there are two additional bids available. Here is a neat scheme:

1♣-1♠*-2♦-2♥	Good raise in ♣ (having denied a ♥-suit already)
→ → → 2♠	Good raise in ♦ (having denied a ♠-suit already)
→ → → 3♣	Weak raise in ♣
→ → → 3♦	Weak raise in ♦

In some other sequences there is less room but still enough to make a difference: For example, after a 1♣-1♠*-2♥ start:

1♣-1♠*-2♥-2♠	Good raise in ♣ (having denied a ♠-suit already)
→ → → 3♣	Weak raise in ♣

Opener's reverse after responder has replied with a natural 1NT also provides some leg room if responder prefers opener's minor:

1♦-1N-2♥-2♠	Good raise in ♦ (having denied a ♠-suit already)
→ → → 3♦	Weak raise in ♦

The impossible major as a good raise of opener's minor is available not only after a reverse by opener but also when she rebids a lower ranking suit after responder's 1NT:

1♥-1N-2♦-2♠	Good raise in ♦ (having denied a ♠-suit already)
→ → → 3♦	Weak raise in ♦

So, generally, responder's rebid of a previously denied major is a very useful proxy as a good raise of opener's minor, differentiating it from a weaker direct raise.

I like to treat all the above as additions to my normal response system after partner reverses. Incidentally, the negative reply to a reverse in my normal system in all other situations after 3 suits had been mentioned is to bid the cheaper of 2NT and the fourth suit (Bourke's relay) to show weakness and inability to prefer partner's first suit or raise his second.

5.5 Weak jump shifts

Weak jump shifts are a very effective species. They paint responder's hand very specifically, showing precisely a 6-card suit and values below that of an opening hand, in other words a hand which would have opened a weak-2 had the responder been first to speak.

So, 1♦-2♥ or 1♦-2♠ describes a responder's hand with a 6-card major in the 5-8 HCP range (not 9 or 10 HCP for reasons which will become clear very shortly).

Similarly after a 1♣ opening. In fact there is even more going for weak jump shifts after a 1♣ opening given the twist of transfer responses and the specific 3-way jump-transfer response feature which were discussed on page 57 in Transfer Responses to 1♣. So:

1♣*-2♣*   Either weak-2 in ♦; Or ♦ single-suited game-force; Or ♣/♦ jump-fit

1♣*-2♦*   Either weak-2 in ♥; Or ♥ single-suited game-force; Or ♣/♥ jump-fit

1♣*-2♥*   Either weak-2 in ♠; Or ♠ single-suited game-force; Or ♣/♠ jump-fit

Although mostly used as a tool after a minor suit opening, the principle applies equally after a 1♥ opening when responder has a weak-two in spades. so 1♥-2♠ showing a 6-card spade suit and 5-8 HCP.

We are talking about only 2-level jump responses to 1-level openings, so there are no weak jump responses at the 3-level in a lower ranking suit.

The system applies in the same way whether responder was a passed hand or was yet to speak.

If the first opponent intervenes with a double the system applies just the same. if not more so.

Indeed the system also applies if the first opponent overcalls at the 1-level but the overcall does not disturb the system. The relevant sequences are 1m-(1♥)-2♠ and 1♣-(1♦)-2M.

I have suggested the range of 5-8 HCP for the weak jump shifts. This is so that the alternative of bidding slowly in two steps to the 2-level can now specifically show the 9-10 HCP range and a 6-card suit. So. for example. 1♦-1♥-1NT-2♥ can now be distinguished as a 9-10 HCP response.

Faced with an immediate 5-8 HCP weak jump shift response, opener will nearly always simply complete the jump-transfer with most hands. And responder will nearly always pass the completion, except with the strong alternative imbedded in the 3-way responses after a 1♣ opening.

In order to make a unilateral further move opener needs considerable additional values and/or fit (much more so than when facing, for example, an opening weak-2 bid or its equivalent via multi-2♦).

But on the occasions when opener does have that power-house to make another move, she still has 2NT available as an Ogust-type enquiry. Straight-forward replies (rather than any inversion of the order) are best when the original response had already shown a narrower than usual range (5-8 HCP) and I suggest the following:

1♦- 2♠	Weak-2 in spades, 5-8 HCP and 6-card suit
→ → 2N	Big opening hand, Ogust-type enquiry anchoring in spades
→ → → 3♣	Lower range, with 1 of top 3 honours
→ → → 3♦	Lower range, with 2 of top 3 honours
→ → → 3♥	Higher range, with 1 of top 3 honours
→ → → 3♠	Higher range, with 2 of top 3 honours
→ → → 3N	AKxxxx in the anchor suit

Chapter 6

Major Suit Sequences

There is a lot that rides on finding and making the most of our major suit fits. The 5-card suit opening bid in a major is already a good start which we can build on.

We already discussed responder's approach when he holds a game-forcing hand with or without support for opener's major. Without repeating our discussion in Chapter 2, let's try to go about things in this section here in terms of the hand types with which we are seeking to raise partner's 1M opening bid.

6.1   3-card raises

I prefer a single raise with all 3-card fits in the traditional 6-9 HCP range (rather than some of those going through the wide range 1NT response).

With 3 trumps and 10-11 HCP, responder uses the wide range 1NT to start with but at his next turn jumps to 3 of partner's suit (1♠-1NT-2♣-3♠).

With 3 trumps and 12-13 HCP, responder makes an initial 2-over-1 response and then jumps to game in partner's suit as a delayed game-raise (1♠-2♣-2NT-4♠). Responder's approach here demostrates the fast-arrival principle and alerts opener not to expect any extras for responder's original force to game.

With 3 trumps and 14+ HCP, responder makes an initial 2-over-1 response and then makes a minimum rebid in partner's suit (1♠-2♣-2NT-3♠). This slow approach brings out the benefits of the system by now giving opener room to make an informative new bid enabling the partnership to judge slam prospects, all below game.

6.2   Bergenish raises

With 4 trumps, up to 6 HCP but a distributional hand, responder raises to 3-level, the level of the 9-card fit between the two hands. 4-level is similarly justified with 5-card support.

With 4+ trumps and 7-9 HCP responder raises to 3♦ and with 10-11 HCP he raises to 3♣. My suggested two bids here are the other way around to Marty Bergen's original formulation of this convention. In case opener has a marginal hand that is worth a game-try I prefer her to have some room to make an encouraging invitational or last-train bid over the 10-11 HCP responder hand type and this inversion of 3♣ and 3♦ bids helps.

If hearts are trumps, opener would have no invitational step at all if responder were to have to bid 3♦ to show 10-11 HCP as in the original Bergen. Even with my suggested inversion when responder bids 3♣ instead, opener has only one step available (3♦). That one step has to serve as a general purpose last train encouragement for game and not necessarily a diamond cue-bid. If spades are trumps then opener, when not signing off, has a choice of two bids and he can bid the better-controlled suit as a game-invitation.

With 4+ trumps and 12+ HCP, my tool of choice is a Jacoby 2NT response to partner's 1M opening bid. I will discuss this further below.

To sum up the Bergenish sequences for the moment, here are the options of an unpassed responder when partner opens 1M:

1M-2M	6-9 HCP with 3 card fit (if doubled → Transfer responses)
1M-2NT	Jacoby GF with 4+ card support (→ see Jacoby sequences)
1M-3♣	10-11 HCP with 4+ card support
1M-3♦	7-9 HCP with 4+ card support
1M-3M	Pre-emptive 4+ card support

6.3   Passed hand Bergen

If already a passed hand the responder by definition is not in a position to force to game any more and so an immediate 2NT response here to partner's 1M opening is best played as a natural 11 HCP raise with not more than 2 cards in opener's major.

1♥-2NT also denies spades. 1♠-2NT may however include a 4-card heart suit although responder should probably avoid this sequence if he has a plausible alternative, so that any 4-4 heart fit does not get overlooked.

If we remember that passed hands with 10-11 HCP and 3 or 4-card fit for partner's major need to go through Drury 2♣, then we do not need the usual 3♣ Bergen raise for a 4-card fit in the 10-11 HCP range any more. In that case we can shift down the remaining Bergen raises. We still need a bid for a 7-9 HCP 4-card raise, which used to be 3♦ for an unpassed hand, but that can now be shifted-down to 3♣ for a passed-hand, so that we create just a little more room for opener to make invitational bids even facing an originally passed partner.

Thus, these are the options for a passed hand responder with a fit for partner's 1M opening bid:

P-1M-2M   6-9 HCP with 3 card fit (if doubled → see Transfer responses)

P-1M-3♣   7-9 HCP with 4+ card fit (passed-hand Bergen shifting down)

P-1M-2NT   Natural 11 HCP (→ see Drury 2♣ for 3+ card fit with 10-11 HCP)

6.4 Jacobyish 2NT raise

I said that with 4+ trumps and 12+ HCP, responder makes a game-forcing Jacoby-2NT response. This of course is relevant only to unpassed responder hands because a passed hand by definition could not have opening values.

Following responder's 2NT. Oswald Jacoby's original scheme envisaged a new suit by opener at 3-level as a splinter and at 4-level as a good second 5-card suit.

I prefer to switch those rebids the other way around. I associate a jump to the 4-level with a splinter more readily, as with most other splinter bids. This leaves 3-level bids in new suits to show a 4+card second suit in a better-than-minimum hand.

Minimum opening hands do best to bid game in the major immediately, in accordance with the fast arrival principle when there is nothing to add.

This leaves an opener's rebid at 3-level. which I like to play as showing a 6th card in the suit and a better-than-minimum hand. leaving room to explore slam possibilities below game-level.

Finally, there is also a 3NT rebid available for opener (1M-2NT-3NT) and we have only the 18-19 HCP hand types remaining to describe and so this fits well here. We would of course never choose to play in 3NT as a final contract when we are aware of our 9 card fit in a major. This 3NT rebid also suitably coincides with the 'serious 3NT' idea, to be more fully discussed on page 204 in Fine-tuning. which confirms that opener is serious about slam prospects and invites responder to cue-bid.

So. my modified Jacoby 2NT continuations can be summarised as follows:

1M-2NT	Jacoby: game forcing raise with 1+ card support	
→ → 3M	6th card in Major. better than minimum	
→ → 3other	4+ card side suit. better than minimum	
→ → 3NT	18-19 HCP. balanced	
→ → 4M	Minimum	
→ → 4other	Splinter (does not promise extra values)	

6.5   Two-tiered splinters

With 4+ trumps and a side suit void or singleton. responder has the perfect hand for a splinter raise when partner opens 1M.

The first thing to be said here is that splinter responder hands work best if they are limited to a defined point range. which should not be set too high or too wide. With very good hands responder can always start with a 2/1 game-forcing bid and take it slowly and allow opener to describe her hand and so assess slam prospects allowing for his own singleton or void.

At the same time. the splintering responder hand should have enough high card points to guarantee game. So. I suggest 11-14 HCP range in pure high card points for immediate splinter responses to partner's

1M opening bid.

It is possible to have two types of splinter bids available in the response structure to communicate two different hand types. One series could be the usual double-jump splinter bids naming the void or singleton suit. Another series could start with a cipher bid, such as 1♠-3NT, to annouce the fact of some splinter, which then needs a relay to allow responder to name the splinter suit if opener wants to know it.

There are a variety of two-tiered splinter schemes one can play. One scheme is to differentiate more specifically between a singleton on the one hand and a void on the other. I think that this may be a duplication of methods if we also have other ways of identifying voids in subsequent bidding, for example in our RKCB sequences as we will see on page 160 in Blackwood Collection.

I prefer differentiating between splinter hand types by further splitting the point range into smaller sub-ranges, 11-12 HCP and 13-14 HCP. So the full range of responder's two-tiered splinter over partner's 1M opening bid would as follows:

1♥- 3N/4♣/4♦	13-14 pure HCP with splinter in ♠/♣/♦
1♥- 3♠	11-12 HCP with unspecified splinter
→ → 3N	Name your splinter (→ 4♥ reply acts as proxy for ♠ splinter)
1♠- 4♣/♦/♥	13-14 pure HCP with splinter as named
1♠- 3NT	11-12 HCP with unspecified splinter
→ → 4♣	Name your splinter (→ 4♠ reply acts as proxy for ♣ splinter)

6.6   If they overcall our 1M opening bid

If the first opponent overcalls our 1M opening bid then this provides
an opportunity for a responder with a fit to differentiate between a
good raise and a weak raise.

All direct raises are pre-emptive after their intervening overcall and
our 3♣ or 3♦ Bergen raises no longer apply (and they may have
overcalled in one of those suits after all).

With a good hand it works best if responder immediately
distinguishes his degree of fit when he has a fit. We would not hold
back from bidding to the 3-level even when we have only an 8-card
fit when responder has a good hand and so he cue-bids opponents'
suit with 3-card support and bids 2NT with 4-card support. This
2NT does not say anything about stoppers in the overcalled suit
because we would not choose to play in no-trumps when we have a
9-card major suit fit.

A jump to 3NT by responder would be to play and it denies 3-card
support.

Remember that 2-over-1 methods no longer apply when the first
opponent overcalls and so our side reverts to our otherwise agreed
normal methods. So, in the absence of a fit, responder would bid a
natural 1NT or 2-level suit, unless passing for real or as a trap.

So, after partner opens 1M and the first opponent overcalls,
responder's more systematic responses are as follows:

1M-(overcall)-2M	Weak raise with 3 card support
1M-(overcall)-3M	Weak raise with 4 card support
1M-(overcall)-Cue	Good raise or better with 3 card support
1M-(overcall)-2NT	Good raise or better with 4+ card support
1M-(overcall)-3NT	To play, with less than 3 card support

6.7 Transfer responses when our 1M opening bid is doubled

When partner's 1♥ or 1♠ opening bid is doubled by the first opponent for takeout, the following transfer structure by responder works well:

1♥- (x)-1♠	This one is not a transfer: Shows 4+spades, 6+HCP, normal
→ → 1N*	Shows 6+ clubs in weak hand or 4+ clubs in good hand
→ → 2♣*	Shows 6+ diamonds weak hand or 5+ diamonds good hand
→ → 2♦*	Shows a good raise to 2♥, about 7-9 HCP, 3 card support
→ → 2♥*	Shows a weak raise to 2♥, about 4-6 HCP, 3 card support

1♠- (x)-1N*	Shows 6+ clubs in weak hand or 4+ clubs in good hand
→ → 2♣*	Shows 6+ diamonds weak hand or 4+ diamonds good hand
→ → 2♦*	Shows 6+ hearts in weak hand or 5+ hearts in good hand
→ → 2♥*	Shows a good raise to 2♠, about 7-9 HCP, 3 card support
→ → 2♠*	Shows a weak raise to 2♠, about 4-6 HCP, 3 card support

Pass, redouble and higher level responses retain their usual meanings.

There are several advantages to the above transfer structure. Firstly, a transfer to a new suit allows responder to show a modest hand with a long suit, even below the usual 10+ HCP requisite for a 2-level response. So for example he can now bid with a 7+ HCP hand and a 6-card suit.

Unless holding a big hand, opener should simply complete the transfer (which does not show fit and could be a singleton or even a void) and responder can pass this out. The benefit will come when responder has an invitational, or even a strong hand, in which case he will continue over partner's completion of the transfer with a descriptive new bid. This could be: another suit; Hx 'fit' in opener's major; a jump-invite with 3-card fit; a cue bid as a stopper-asking enquiry, etc.

Secondly, the opening hand, usually the bigger hand, will be declaring the contract if we buy it and the lead will now be coming away from the doubling, stronger opponent.

Thirdly, with a 3-card fit for opener but a limited hand, responder now has two ways of raising opener's major to the 2-level: directly with 4-6 HCP and by transfer with 7-9 HCP.

Fourthly, if the second opponent competes, we do not lose anything and may now even gain as two new bids (pass and double) also become available to opener.

Fifthly, even if the opponents buy the auction, responder will have indicated his best assets which could be a good side suit for opener to lead.

The disadvantage is the surrender of a natural 1NT response over the double. But I rather think that the gain of the several advantages listed above more than compensates for that loss.

Any response below 1NT remains natural (in effect the 1♥-(x)-1♠ sequence) so we do not get talked out of a spade-fit our way in case their double did not promise spades.

This system applies only when partner opens in a major. It does not apply if our 4+ card 1♦ opening bid is doubled for takeout and we have our more extensive transfer responses if our 2+ card 1♣ opening bid is doubled. In minor suit cases we also retain our inverted raises after a double or any other intervention, as we discussed on page 65 in Minor Suit Sequences.

6.8   Responder's 2NT rebid as game-force after major-suit agreement

Normally responder does not have a clearly game-forcing rebid after opener's agreement to his suit in a sequence such as 1♦-1♥-2♥ or similar.

Interestingly, there are ways for responder to invite game in such cases. For example: a new suit would be a long-suit trial bid; a rebid by responder in opener's original minor would typically show a fitting honour in a 3-card fit there (1♦-1♥-2♥-3♦); and a raise of the agreed major could be a general game-try.

But is there also a way for responder to set a clear game-force? It seems not. No matter. I have a concoction of my own to deal with this problem.

It seems to me that a 2NT continuation after a major suit agreement is largely redundant because we would normally choose to play in our major suit fit. So I think that 2NT could be used artificially to cover all game-forcing hands (1♦-1♥-2♥-2NT). Responder is of course still unlimited here although opener is probably marked with 12-15 HCP. With any more than that. opener would have jump-raised responder's major.

In response to the 2NT game-force. opener could now clarify her range. and whether she raised on a 3-card or 4-card fit. and perhaps even a little more about her hand-shape.

Opener would have rebid 1NT in the first place with a weak-NT type hand and 3-card support. so the above scheme now systemically allows for a 3-card raise with a side suit shortage and/or with length in opener's original minor.

It seems sensible to reserve the 3-level replies below 3 of the agreed major to show a 3-card raise and at the same time re-define opener's range:

1♦- 1♥- 2♥- 2N	Game-force with hearts agreed
→ → → → 3♣	3-card raise with minimum hand (12-13 HCP)
→ → → → 3♦	3-card raise but with values to spare (14-15 HCP)

When trumps are spades (1♦-1♠-2♠-2NT). there is also a 3♥ rebid available which provides a choice of red suit features for the upper range opener to show.

All higher responses by opener, starting with 3 of the agreed major, show four cards support and pinpoint her hand shape in other respects. I like 3M and 4M to show no-shortage but redefine opener's strength between a hand with extra-values (3M) or a minimum (fast-arrival 4M). But any new suit bid by opener can now show a shortage, whereas a rebid of opener's original minor (obviously not a shortage) could instead show a semi-solid source of tricks there. When showing a shortage (or a semi-solid original minor) opener can also split her range in the style of the two-tier splinters I discussed earlier.

So, 4-card fit continuations when hearts were agreed become:

1♦- 1♥- 2♥- 2N	Game-force with hearts agreed
→ → → → 1♥	4-card fit, minimum (fast arrival), maybe no shortage
→ → → → 3♥	4-card fit, maximum, maybe no shortage
→ → → → 3♠	4-card fit, 12-13 HCP with an unspecified splinter
→ → → → → 3N	Name your splinter (→ 4♥reply shows ♠-splinter)
→ → → → 3N	4-card fit, 14-15 HCP with ♠-splinter
→ → → → 1♣	4-card fit, 14-15 HCP with ♣-splinter
→ → → → 1♦	4-card fit, 14-15 HCP, semi-solid first suit of opener

4-card fit continuations when spades were agreed are similar:

1♦- 1♠- 2♠- 2N	Game-force with spades agreed
→ → → → 4♠	4-card fit, minimum (fast arrival), maybe no shortage
→ → → → 3♠	4-card fit, maximum, maybe no shortage
→ → → → 3N	4-card fit, 12-13 HCP with an unspecified splinter
→ → → → → 4♣	Name your splinter (→ 4♠reply shows ♣-splinter)
→ → → → 4♣	4-card fit, 14-15 HCP with ♣-splinter
→ → → → 4♦	4-card fit, 14-15 HCP, semi-solid first suit of opener
→ → → → 4♥	4-card fit, 14-15 HCP with ♥-splinter

This two-tier response structure is akin to our two-tier splinter raises of partner's 1M opening bid which we discussed on page 80 earlier in this chapter, except that this time we have two splinter suits or a semi-solid original minor suit to show, rather than three splinter suits. But the lower and higher points range differentiation is equally available. If holding both a splinter and a semi-solid previous minor, I suggest that opener chooses to show the splinter.

All the above examples were based on a 1♦ opening bid for convenience but apply equally after a 1♥ or a 1♣ opening bid, in the latter case allowing also for transfer responses.

How often would opener rebid 1NT in the first place instead of raising responder's major with 3-card support? Well, with most undistinguished weak-NT type hands opener would rebid 1NT despite 3-card fit. So, the availability of the continuations we discussed here means that we can now systemically allow for a 3-card raise of responder's major when opener has a side suit shortage and/or length in her original minor.

Chapter 7

1NT Sequences

Our opening 1NT range is 15-17 HCP. Before I say more about that it is worth recapping on our bids with balanced hands outside this range.

With 12-14 HCP. we open one of a suit and rebid in no-trumps at the lowest available level; so 1NT after a 1-level response and 2NT after a 2-level response.

With 18-19 HCP. we open one of a suit and this time rebid 2NT irrespective of whether partner responds at 1-level or 2-level. If partner responds at 1-level then our jump rebid in no-trumps clearly shows extra strength. so 18-19 HCP. That is clear enough.

If on the other hand our opening bid of 1♦ or 1♥ or 1♠ brings out a 2-level initial response from partner then we are already in a 2-over-

1 sequence forcing to game. In this case there is no need to jump to show our extra strength any more, which is an exception with balanced hands only, and so here we still simply rebid 2NT. This therefore is a dual range rebid, showing 12-14 HCP or 18-19 HCP. Partner will initially assume 12-14 HCP but we can clarify our extra strength later by bidding on when partner stops.

With 20+ HCP balanced hands I strongly believe in 2-point ranges because with 3-point ranges it becomes necessary to incorporate invitational bids into the system and there is often not enough bidding space after a 2-level start in the first place. So, our system envisages the following structure for stronger balanced-hands:

- With 20-21 HCP, open multi-2♦ and rebid 2NT;

- With 22-23 HCP, use the sequence 2♣-2♦-2NT;

- With 24-25 HCP, use the sequence 2♣-2♦-2♥-2♠-2NT

The strong balanced hands will be discussed in detail in Chapter 12. For now let's concentrate on 1NT sequences.

7.1 1NT shape considerations

I believe in a practical approach to opening the bidding with 1NT, an approach which should be more about the range and less about the shape.

As far as the range is concerned, I cannot think of any good reason to diverge from the requirement to hold 15-17 HCP in the first and second positions. There may be some excuse in the third and fourth seat to open with a good 14 HCP but preferably there should be some compensating feature such as a decent 5-card suit because partner should still always be entitled to assume a 15-17 HCP range and respond accordingly.

As far as the shape is concerned, the balanced hand constraint is too narrow for me. I like my 1NT opener to include not only the semi-balanced hand type but where the circumstances dictate even some atypical hands.

I have no qualms about having a 6-card minor or for that matter a singleton minor in my 1NT. Not every single one that comes around but only those hands with a good 6-card minor suit in the 15-17 HCP range where the other three suits are reasonably protected.

The singleton minor can never be any singleton; it needs to be preferably the Ace or at least the King. For instance a 4-4-1-4 or 4-4-4-1 hand in the 15-17 HCP range is fine as a 1NT opener for me, not least because it is very problematic to bid it otherwise.

It goes without saying that hands with a 5-card suit are perfectly fine for opening 1NT, including a 5-card major. This used to be a cardinal sin in some people's Standard-American but thankfully attitudes have been changing. With some hands there is simply no better bid to get out the general message about the fairly balanced nature of the hand in that HCP range in one single shot. Any other start will usually leave your subsequent bids with less precision because they then have to cover more hand types and wider ranges.

I don't even mind if my 1NT opener has to include a 4-card suit alongside a 5-card suit. It would be rare but there is sometimes no better alternative when the 4-card suit is higher ranking, the hand is not strong enough for a reverse rebid and the 2-card suits have stoppers. If not opening 1NT with these hands then another sequence may not do justice to, say, a 16 HCP hand with that shape.

Partner needs to be alert to the possibility of somewhat less-balanced 1NT openers. So, if opener comes back into the bidding at 2-level after opponents intervene then this will no doubt be opener's 5-card major in her original 1NT. Equally, if the opponents negotiate a penalty double, opener will no doubt want to retreat to a 6-card minor.

7.2   Breaking transfers

The rationale for playing transfers over partner's 1NT opening bid is well established and universally played. The main reason is that it pays to set up opener as declarer because that tends to be the bigger hand and so best not to reveal it entirely as dummy. Also the bigger hand normally has more tenaces to protect against the opening lead.

The other practical advantage is that the relay gives the transferor another bid, which can often be put to good alternative uses if he is not passing out the completion of the transfer. For instance he can make an invitational rebid or show a second suit, etc.

By the same logic, additional advantages can be gained if the transferee also makes some alternative bids with appropriate hands rather than routinely complete the transfer the same way each time.

It goes without saying that the 1NT opener has no choice when she does not like the suit to which responder is transferring; she simply has to complete the transfer - unless of course there is an intervention by the opponent in which case opener can now pass the bidding back to responder to indicate her dislike of the transfer request.

But when the opener/transferee does like the sound of the transfer it is incumbent upon her to communicate her enthusiasm. After all that may be all the encouragement the responder/transferor needs to bid on to game.

If an opponent intervenes over the transfer request then the transferee's voluntarily completion of the transfer shows a 3-card fit given that she did not have to bid at all after the intervention.

With or without any intervention there ought to be much more the transferee can do when she has as good a fit for the intended suit as a 4-card fit or even a 5-card fit.

Over a transfer request into a major suit I like to jump-complete the transfer at the 3-level when I have a 4-card fit for the major and 15-16 HCP. 9-card fit justifies the 3-level (law of total tricks) even with a minimum NT-opener and a weak responder hand.

But with maximum 17 HCP along with the 4-card fit, it works well to break the transfer to show a suit with a poor doubleton in order that responder can judge game potential in borderline situations. Bidding 2NT instead denies a poor doubleton but still 17 HCP, which may be equally useful information for partner.

In the unlikely case of 5-card support for responder's indicated major there is no reason to hold back at all. Even with 15-16 HCP, I like to double-jump and complete the transfer at game level. With 17 HCP I like 3NT which is an unusual enough break that even if partner does not immediately recognise it he will work out by logic and elimination that this odd break must be the remaining case of maximum support and maximum points.

As far as transfers into minor suits are concerned, first of all, let's recap that 1NT-2♠ is a transfer to clubs and 1NT-2NT is a transfer to diamonds. I like this arrangement because it leaves an in-between step to give a reply with an alternative meaning.

It works best to play that actually completing a minor suit transfer shows a liking for it, specifically Axx or Kxx or Qxx or of course a better fit, which should be perfect for 3NT.

That leaves the option of short-breaking into the in-between step to show the alternative and deny such a good fit.

This arrangement has the additional benefit that with both minors and a weak hand the transferor bids 2NT, evidently wanting a transfer to diamonds, but if he hears 3♣ back to show partner's dislike for diamonds then he will no doubt do better to simply pass 3♣.

7.3   Responder's options with both majors

If responder is blessed with both majors, he has to make the most of this when partner opens 1NT.

If responder is 4-4 in the majors, unless he is very weak (in which case he will pass), it is very straight forward in that he would make a 2♣ enquiry and take it from there. We will discuss Stayman more particularly in Chapter 8.

If responder is 6-4, it may depend on the relative substance of the two suits. But most of the time you would start with a transfer to the longer major first but then also bring in the shorter major. If there is a 4-4 fit there, the longer major will bury many side suit losers.

There is more to consider when it comes to responder's hands with 4-5, 5-4 or 5-5 in the majors. Here, it is best to further divide the responding hands by strength: weak, intermediate or game-going.

With weak 4-5 and 5-4 hands, I prefer simply to transfer into the 5-card major and play there without further ado. In particular, I do not like junk-Stayman because I like to keep my 2♣ as a constructive enquiry bid.

With weak 5-5 in the majors, there is another small decision to make. Either transfer to the better major and leave it there; or if the heart suit is somewhat better and the hand is borderline anyway then upgrade it to an invitational hand with 4 spades and 5 hearts.

With invitational 4-5 hands, you can first transfer to hearts and then also show spades, still keeping to the 2-level.

The other way around, with invitational 5-4 hands, it is necessary to start with 2♣, which is an exception among invitational hands with both majors. If partner shows up with a 4-card or a 5-card major then all is well. If partner replies 2NT, showing no majors and only

15-16 HCP, then you leave it there and play 2NT. If partner replies 3♣ or 3♦, still no majors but 17 HCP, as we will see on page 105 in Puppet Stayman your 3♥ will now specifically show 5 hearts and 4 spades and you will proceed to game.

With invitational 5-5 hands, transfer to spades and rebid hearts. The 3-level hearts rebid in this book's system is specifically invitational, not forcing as in most other systems. This exception helps to make it possible to show all the different hand types within the overall logic of the present system.

With game-going hands, whether 4-5 or 5-4 or 5-5, responder starts with 2♣. If partner owns up to a 4-card or a 5-card major then again all is well. If partner has no majors and replies 2NT (15-16 HCP) or 3-minor (17 HCP), responder introduces his 5-card major at the 3-level which bid is now game-forcing and also shows at least 4 cards in the other major.

If partner does not even have a 3-card fit for your 5-card major and attempts to sign off in 3NT, then you pass with 4-5 and 5-4 in the majors, but continue bidding out your majors with a 5-5 shape. With 5-5, responder bids spades first and then rebids in hearts. He will not be 6-5 in the majors for bidding like this because with that shape he would transfer in the first place rather than start with 2♣ over 1NT.

It is useful to have a partnership understanding that despite many possible off-shape hand patterns for an initial 1NT opening bid these should not include 2-2 in the majors, so a 1NT opener should have at least one 3-card major. That is not too much to ask. This becomes relevant if responder has 5-5 shape in the majors in a game going hand, with which he should be free to insist on a major suit contract (1NT-2♣-2NT-3♠-3NT-4♥).

Here's a summary of responder's options with both majors facing 1NT:

Weak 4-5 or 5-4:	Transfer to 5-card major to play (no 'junk-Stayman')
Weak 5-5:	Either transfer to better major or treat as invitational 4-5
Invitational 4-5:	Transfer to hearts and rebid spades, keeping to 2-level
Invitational 5-4:	Start with 2♣; pass 2N reply; bid 3♠ over 3m showing 5-4
Invitational 5-5:	Transfer to spades and rebid hearts at 3-level, non-forcing
Game-going 4-5:	Start with 2♣; bid 3♥ over 2N or 3m, showing 4-5, forcing
Game-going 5-4:	Start with 2♣; bid 3♠ over 2N or 3m, showing 5-4+, forcing
Game-going 5-5:	Start with 2♣; bid 3♠ over 2N or 3m, forcing (and rebid 4♥)

7.4   Other 1NT sequences

Let's complete this section with some other less frequent sequences over partner's 1NT opening bid.

Transferring into a major and rebidding a minor (1NT-2♥-2♠-3♦) is forcing a third bid out of opener but is not necessarily forcing to game. A false preference to 3♠ is opener's weakest possible reply, perhaps on a 2-4-3-4 hand pattern and minimum 15-16 HCP.

Transferring into a major and then rebidding 4NT (1NT-2♥-2♠-4NT) is not RKCB for hearts; it is quantitative and seeks opener to choose between 6♥ and 6NT if maximum.

Responder's slam-try is available through an initial jump bid to the 3-level, both with a major or a minor suit (1NT-3♠ or 1NT-3♦). Opener can agree by cue-bidding a side suit or discourage by bidding 3NT. A subsequent 4NT would be RKCB for responder's suit even overruling any initial discouragement by opener (for example 1NT-3♠-3NT-4NT).

Regular RKCB applies when a major suit slam-try is involved (1NT-3♠-3NT-4NT) whereas a minor suit slam try rolls into the more specific minor-suit RKCB (MSRKCB) with 1NT-3♦-3NT-4♦. We will see MSRKCB in more detail on page 162 in Blackwood Collection.

Responder can also transfer into a minor and rebid 4-minor as MSRKCB for that minor irrespective of whether opener completes the initial transfer (to show liking for that minor) or short-break the transfer (to show dislike). Indeed by transferring to diamonds and regardless of opener's reply rebidding 4♣, responder would be showing at least 5-5 in the minors in a slam-going hand whilst the 4♣ bid at the same time starts MSRKCB for clubs (although he may still choose to declare in diamonds later).

1NT-4NT is quantitative as usual although, unless holding a 2-2-5-4 or 2-2-4-5 hand pattern, responder would normally investigate a major suit fit first.

I like to keep the immediate jump to 4 of a major as natural (1NT-4♥ or 4♠) for cases where responder perceives a possible advantage to play the hand, maybe to prevent the initial lead coming through a Kx in a side suit.

1NT-4♣ can remain a Gerber bid, asking for the number of Aces held in steps (starting with 0). with no suit set. After opener's reply a 4NT rebid by responder would be to play and 5♣ would ask for Kings on the same step principle.

Chapter 8

2♣ Puppet Stayman

Most people play 5-card Puppet Stayman over a 2NT opening bid. There the main reason is that the 2NT opening bid can include some less balanced hands and so it is important to identify especially a 5-card major if there is one. not just a 4-card major.

But those are exactly the same issues with the shape of our 1NT openers which I discussed on page 90 in 1NT Sequences. So why not play 5-card Puppet Stayman over 1NT. too?

Indeed. the availability of a 2♣ enquiry to identify a 5-card major with the opener should also help overcome any residual reservation about including a 5-card major in our 1NT hand patterns in the first place.

2♣ as Puppet Stayman works well in practice. In fact you can do more in your Puppet sequences over 1NT because there is more room to describe opener's hand. When a 4-4 major-suit fit is located there is still room for opener to indicate or deny a maximum NT-opener.

Responder should not embark on 2♣ at all unless he has a good 7 or 8 HCP. enough to play at least 2NT because this is what opener may be rebidding in the absence of a 4 or 5-card major. A consequence of this is that there is no 'junk-Stayman' option with my 2♣ for the purpose of bailing out to some suit when responder is weak and 3-suited with shortage in clubs.

Quantitative raises of 1NT to 2NT also go through 2♣. So, responder's initial 2♣ enquiry does not promise a major; he may only be intending to invite 3NT if opener has the maximum 17 HCP hand.

8.1 When 1NT opener reveals a 5-card major

If responder does not have a 4-card major he should still be alert to the possibility that opener may have a 5-card major. So, responder should investigate a 5-3 fit when he has only a 3-card major or two 3-card majors in his own hand.

After a 1NT-2♣ start, opener bids a 5-card major if she has one. This is the most straight-forward situation. If an immediate major suit fit comes to light, more likely a 5-3 fit and occasionally a 5-4 fit, then responder can take control.

With opener's range already well defined along with the news now of a 5-card fitting major, responder's options include an invitational raise (1NT-2♣-2♥-3♥) or jump to game (1NT-2♣-2♥-4♥). A jump to 4NT by responder (1NT-2♣-2♥-4NT) is not RKCB but a quantitative no-trump raise, asking opener to bid 6NT with maximum 17 HCP for her opening 1NT.

To initiative a RKCB sequence for hearts, responder needs to go via the other major, spades. The other major in these sequences is otherwise a redundant bid but even without discussion it sounds forcing and opener would never pass it even if she is not quite sure where responder is going. Whatever opener says responder then bids 4NT which now serves as an RKCB-asking bid in the first major, the 5-card major earlier revealed by opener. So:

1N- 2♣-2♥- 2♠- any-4N   becomes RKCB for hearts (cancelling the earlier 2♠)

1N- 2♣-2♠- 3♥- any-4N   becomes RKCB for spades (cancelling the earlier 3♥)

Whilst the insertion of the other major after a positive Stayman response subsequently unravels as a RKCB manoeuvre, a 3-level rebid in a minor (1NT-2♣-2♥-3♣ or 3♦) is natural and forcing.

8.2   When 1NT opener reveals a 4-card major

If the NT-opener has only a 4-card major, or two 4-card majors, then he will reply the Puppet enquiry with 2♦ (i.e., 1NT-2♣-2♦).

In order that opener, usually the bigger of the two hands, gets to play any subsequent major suit contract, over opener's 2♦, responder needs to bid the major he does not have. So he bids 2♥ to show 4-card spades or bids 2♠ to show 4-card hearts. This is the Puppet element of the system.

With 4-cards in both hearts and spades, responder initially admits to hearts by bidding 2♠. Subsequent bidding has room for clarification and any spade fit will not be missed.

Once opener gets to know responder's 4-card major her third round bid can now show not only whether partner's major matches with her own but also whether or not she has maximum 17 HCP for her original 1NT. This will help responder to judge the level at which to place the final contract.

Let's see the full sequences for 4-card major scenarios including range-specifications:

1N-2♣-2♦	Opener has at least one 4-card major, no 5-card major
→ → → 2♥	Responder has 4 spades, may also have 4 hearts
→ → → → 2♠	Opener agrees spades, 15-16 HCP
→ → → → 3♠	Opener agrees spades, 17 HCP
→ → → → 2N	Opener denies spades (must have 4 hearts), 15-16 HCP
→ → → → 3N	Opener denies spades (must have 4 hearts), 17 HCP
→ → → 2♠	Responder has 4 hearts, denies 4 spades
→ → → → 2N	Opener denies 4 hearts (must have 4 spades), 15-16 HCP
→ → → → 3N	Opener denies 4 hearts (must have 4 spades), 17 HCP
→ → → → 3♥	Opener agrees hearts: 15-16 HCP
→ → → → 4♥	Opener agrees hearts: 17 HCP

8.3 When 1NT opener has no majors

Following the 1NT-2♣ start, opener bids 2NT holding neither a 5-card nor a 4-card major suit and with 15-16 HCP, not maximum, for her opening bid.

Earlier I raised a prerequisite that responder's initial 2♣ enquiry should not be made on every hand but that this needs to be a constructive move with at least a good 7 HCP and preferably no less than 8 HCP. On that basis, when opener denies a major, 2NT as an eventual contract should present no problem.

If on that basis responder has at least invitational values then when opener does not have a major suit feature to show, she can afford to reply beyond 2NT with maximum 17 HCP. So, she can use 1NT-2♣-3♣ or 3♦ to show the better/longer of her minors whilst announcing a maximum hand for her original 1NT albeit without a major. If not for this 3-level break by opener, a marginal responder lacking room to invite 3NT might be selling out to 2NT. Even 5 of a minor may be making if responder is not so marginal but fittingly distributional.

There is of course still the possibility that responder all along had a big hand of his own when he started the 2♣ enquiry. So whether opener replies with 2NT or 3♣ or 3♦, responder may yet have higher ambitions.

If responder had both majors himself, as we saw on page 96 in 1NT Sequences he would have also initially responded 2♣ holding a game-going hand with 5-5, 5-4 or 4-5 in the majors (and also invitational hands with specifically 5 spades and 4 hearts). So, after opener denies any majors, if responder still introduces a major at the 3-level

this is his 5-card major alongside at least 4 in the other major in a
big hand and opener can raise to game with only 3-card support and
a minimum for her opening 1NT bid but only reply again with 3NT
when she does not have a 3-card fit for responder's named major.

If responder had a big hand with a 4-card major and longer-minor,
he would have equally made a start with 2♣. When opener denies a
major with a 2NT or 3♣ or 3♦ reply, responder then has the means
to change tact and go with his minor. A jump or bid of 4 of a minor
by responder here would be MSRKCB for that minor. This does not
have to match opener's minor if she had mentioned a minor along
the way. So, 1NT-2♣-3♦-4♣ is MSRKCB for clubs as is 1NT-2♣-
3♣-4♣. We discuss MSRKCB in detail on page 162 in Blackwood
Collection.

8.4   If our 2♣ enquiry is doubled

If an opponent doubles our 2♣ Puppet Stayman enquiry I have a
useful gadget as a counter measure. Far from that intervention
inconveniencing us, we can turn it into an advantage.

There is no need to ask the opponents to clarify what their double
of our 2♣ meant. It would only serve to clarify the position more
for them than for us. We can simply assume that the double showed
clubs either as a lead-directing attempt or with a view to competing
in that suit. It does not matter which or neither.

Our original 1NT opener, readying for a reply to the 2♣ Puppet
enquiry, now has an option over their double. She can simply choose
to pass the double and I'm suggesting that a pass here shows club

stopper(s).

This could prove useful in deciding. for example. whether we still choose to play 3NT as a final contract.

What happens when the next opponent almost certainly also passes?

No problem. Responder now redoubles to reconvene our Puppet Stayman sequence. This time our original 1NT opener can have a second bite at the cherry to answer the real question about majors.

The corollary to our opener's stopper-showing pass is that. in the absence of a stopper. she just bids as she would have done had there been no double of the 2♣ enquiry. 2♦ confirms at least one 4-card major. 2♥ or 2♠ shows a 5-card major. etc. but this time specifically without a club stopper.

So any voluntary continuation over the double. rather than conventionally passing it. now becomes a dual-meaning bid which in addition to the usual meaning now also deny a club stopper. Neat, isn't it?

Chapter 9

Interference With Our 1NT

It is important to have firm agreements in place to deal with opponents' interventions with our 1NT opening bid and/or our responder's replies.

If there is a rare natural 2♣ overcall by the first opponent (or a 2-suited or even a Cansino-style 3-suited overcall which includes clubs as one of the suits) then responder is not particularly inconvenienced. He can double, meaning that he was going to bid this himself artificially as our usual Puppet Stayman enquiry. In all other respects of our system he can also still bid exactly as he was going to do, including transfers.

If there is a penalty-double of our 1NT opening bid by the first opponent then responder is still not inconvenienced. He can do

everything just as before simply ignoring the double. In addition
there is now a redouble available to him, best played as an escape
to a 5+ card minor - so opener takes it out to 2♣ which responder
passes out or corrects to 2♦. These are options which responder
did not have before.

If the second opponent penalty-doubles our 1NT and this comes
round all the way back to our responder. 1NT-(p)-p-(x)-p-(p). then
a wider escape mechanism is possible. A redouble again asks
opener to bid 2♣ which responder will pass or correct to some
other 5-card suit which could conceivably be a major he supressed
earlier. On the other hand a direct suit bid promises only a 4-card
suit but also a second higher ranking 4-card suit in an unbalanced
weak hand. Opener should pass responder's first 4-card suit with a
3-card fit there. failing which she can bid her own 3-card suits
upwards to identify a possibly better fit. Incidentally. this above
escape mechanism is something I also suggest for our advancer if
the opponents penalty-double our 1NT-overcall of their opening
bid.

9.1   Artificial interventions

If an opponent's intervention over our 1NT opening bid is
conventional but nevertheless indicates a specified anchor suit then
it is just as easy for our responder to treat their bidding as if they
actually overcalled in that anchor suit. This frees up responder to
double to show interest in the cipher suit but actually bid their
anchor suit as takeout with a shortage in that suit.

So. if the first opponent overcalls our 1NT with an Astro-style
2♦ showing spades and another. then our responder can: double to

show interest in diamonds; bid 2♥ competitively with 5-hearts; or bid 2♠ as a general take-out of spades with only 4-hearts.

If an opponent's overcall indicates two other equally applicable suits, such as 2♣ Landy showing both majors, strictly speaking this does not inconvenience our responder. However now he will hardly be doubling this overcall as his improvised enquiry for majors or make a transfer bid to a major when the opponents are themselves booked for majors. In this case his double would show interest in competing in clubs. This must remain the case whenever their cipher suit stands for some other two suits.

If an opponent's intervention is in a cipher suit (or is a double) meaning some other yet-to-be-identified single suit, such as a Capelletti-style 2♣ or a Multi-Landy style 2♦, then all our responder can do is wait until the bidding comes round to him again with their suit clarified. Our usual system to deal with interventions will apply thereafter.

If their overcall shows the bid suit and one other non-specific suit then the simplest thing to do is to treat it as just a natural overcall for the time being.

You cannot prepare for every artificial intervention method the opponents may spring up on you but a few general principles in your partnership understandings such as the above will often go a long way even against surprise systems.

9.2   Rubensohl

For dealing with natural interventions with our 1NT (or after artificial interventions are naturalised) Rubensohl seems to be an improvement over the better known Lebensohl methods. It is the same idea in both but a different approach because the priorities are reversed.

The typical problem is when the first opponent overcalls our 1NT with a suit and our responder indicates interest in the proceedings perhaps with a double or articial-2NT but the other opponent raises the stakes, for example in the sequence 1NT-(2♠)-2NT-(3♠), before we have got our act together.

In Lebensohl the 2NT in the above sequence only shows responder's intention to compete but not yet his suit. This is a major drawback for opener who is now none the wiser. Rubensohl, on the other hand, reverses the approach such that responder indicates his suit first.

More specifically, in Rubensohl over the intervention all responder's bids starting from 2NT are transfer bids to the next strain. Now even if the next opponent ups the ante, our opener remains informed.

Furthermore, when the completion of the transfer comes back, responder gets a chance to bid again with suitable forcing hands. So the initial bid can be weak or strong. This latter feature of having two bites at the cherry is also a very useful improvement.

All transfer bids below the rank of the intervention suit should be initially assumed weak. A strong responder will get a second chance with which he can do many things: raise the suit; show a second suit; cue-bid as a stopper-ask; or bid 3NT with a stopper.

Transfers above the rank of the intervention suit are at least invitational. This also means that opener can, in fact must, break the transfer with a suitable maximum hand because in this instance there will not be room to investigate further.

Transfers to the intervention suit itself are Staymanic. If it was a minor then responder would be showing both majors and if it was a major then responder would be showing the other major.

An immediate 3NT by responder denies interest in unbid major(s) and shows stopper(s) in the intervention suit. this being the Fast-Arrival-Shows-Stopper (FASS) principle.

Doubles can now more specifically be penalty doubles catching the overcall suit.

If the opponent's overcall was conventional. Rubensohl can still be played so long as an anchor suit was indicated by the opponent.

It is possible to significantly complicate the continuation bidding to show very many hand types both by responder and opener. However a simple structure for responder, following partner's 1NT opening bid and a natural (or belatedly naturalised) overcall by the opponents, could be as follows:

2-level suit bids	4+card suit, to play
2NT and 3-suit bids below their rank	Transfer to 5+ suit, weak/strong
3-suit bids above their rank	Transfer to 5+ suit, invitational +
3-level transfer to opponent's suit	Stop-ask, Staymanic, game-force
3NT	Denying major(s), showing stop

It is common to play the same methods both when opponents overcall our 1NT and when opponents open a weak-two. But I still prefer Lebensohl as a defence against weak-twos (and their analogous variants) and Rubensohl only when they intervene with our 1NT opening bid where the problems are somewhat different.

Chapter 10

Overcalling Opponents' 1NT

The structure for overcalling opponents' 1NT opening bid which I outline below is not a system you will have come across anywhere. This is because it is basically my own creation.

The emphasis is very much on the majors as you would expect, but it differs from most other majors-orientated methods in many ways. Significantly, ours caters for having one or both majors but in addition it also distinguishes between weak, intermediate or strong overcalls.

The same system can be played against weak or strong no-trumps just with normal due allowance for the relative vulnerability between our side and the opponents.

Equally, the same system can be played in both the direct and protective overcall positions, but naturally the latter can be a little lighter as with all bids in the balancing position.

10.1   Basic system

The basic system is very straightforward:

(1N)-2♣	One or both majors, either weak or strong
(1N)-2♦	Both majors, 4/4+, intermediate
(1N)-2♥/♠	Natural, 5+ card major, intermediate

So, direct 2♥ and 2♠ overcalls are natural and 2♦ overcall shows both majors. All these three are with intermediate values in the 11-15 HCP range.

Everything else goes through 2♣, whether holding one major (6 cards) or both majors (4/4+) and whether weak (6-10 HCP) or strong (16+ HCP). 2♣ is in effect a 6-way bid and it may look as though a lot of hand shapes are loaded into this overcall but this is immediately unravelled.

In response to the 2♣ overcall, initially always assumed weak, advancer bids 2♥ to show ♥-preference but 2♦ as proxy for ♠-preference, both non-forcing responses. With a weak hand the overcaller can then stop at the 2-level by passing partner's 2♥ or converting 2♦ to 2♥ or 2♠. The 'two-under' proxy bid (♦ for ♠) means we find our best fit.

If the 2♣ overcaller had the strong hand type for her overcall whether with one or both majors then she makes a stronger rebid the next time to differentiate.

Let's now see these in more detail in turn. For the rest of this chapter all bids beyond the opponents' 1NT opening belong to our side and their passes are omitted. But the full sequence is given if a second bid or double by the opponents is involved.

10.2   Intermediate overcall hands

I prefer the intermediate 2♥ and 2♠ overcalls to show 5+ cards in the major and not necessarily with any second suit alongside. I find the second suit requirement. even a 4-card minor accompanier, fairly restrictive. The absence of a second suit in some other systems may mean you are unable to overcall with an otherwise perfectly legitimate 5-card major suit. which cannot be right in matchpoints especially against weak no-trumps.

Following a 2♥ or 2♠ overcall. if advancer sees potential for game he can invoke a 2NT enquiry. The overcaller then uses Ogust-style responses to spell out her range and high-card count in the major over 4 steps. as follows:

(1N)-2M	5+ cards in major, intermediate 11-15 HCP, basically natural
→ → 2N	Enquiry
→ → → 3♣	11-13 HCP, 1 of top-3 honours in the major
→ → → 3♦	11-13 HCP, 2 of top-3 honours in the major
→ → → 3♥	14-15 HCP, 1 of top-3 honours in the major
→ → → 3♠	14-15 HCP, 2 of top-3 honours in the major

If our 2♥ or 2♠ overcall is doubled by either opponent whether as takeout or penalty, I see no reason to improvise an escape. Indeed advancer's pass will put any opponent yet to bid under some pressure. But in essence our intermediate overcalls should be good enough to be prepared to play it doubled.

If the overcaller is blessed with both majors in an intermediate hand then even a 4-4 holding is good enough to overcall 2♦. Hopefully more often it will be 5-4. Advancer will usually show simple preference.

But if, following a 2♦ overcall, advancer sees potential for game then he can again invoke a 2NT enquiry. The overcaller can still use Ogust-style responses but this time she also needs to identify if either of the two major suits is longer, as well as splitting her range, so a slightly different set of 4 steps.

So, advancer's full menu this time is more like the following:

(1N)-2♦	Both majors, 4/4+, intermediate, 11-15 HCP
→ → 2♥/♠	Simple preference, not forward-going
→ → 2N	Enquiry
→ → → 3♣	11-13 HCP, longer hearts or equal-length in majors
→ → → 3♦	11-13 HCP, longer spades
→ → → 3♥	14-15 HCP, longer hearts or equal-length in majors
→ → → 3♠	14-15 HCP, longer spades

If our 2♦ overcall is doubled by the next opponent then our advancer does not have to rush into a preference unless one of his majors is notably longer (2+ cards differential) because the overcaller herself may have 5 cards in one major and only 4 in the other.

If the double of 2♦ reaches our overcaller then she simply clarifies her original overcall:

(1N)-2♦-(x)-p-(p)	Advancer passing the double over to overcaller
→ → → → → 2M	Overcaller names her 5-card major if she has one
→ → → → → xx	Overcaller has equal length in majors 4-4 (or 5-5)
→ → → → → → 2M	Advancer chooses

10.3   Weak overcall hands

The rest of this chapter is mostly concerned with sequences starting with a 2♣ overcall, always initially assumed by partner to be weak with one or both majors.

By weak I mean something like a 6-10 HCP hand with a 6-card major when single-suited or at least 4-4 (and ideally 5-4) if holding both majors. This is a fairly aggressive overcall and so when vulnerable we should be at the higher end of the range and our points should be in the major suit(s).

These are the sequences with a weak single-major overcaller and a partner with an undistinguished hand:

(1N)-2♣	One major (6 cards) or both (4/4+), either 6-10 or 16+ HCP
→ → 2♦	Advancer prefers ♠ (3+ cards) [or is 2-1-5-5], non-forcing
→ → → 2♥	Overcaller had a weak 6-card ♥-suit
→ → → 2♠	Overcaller had a weak 6-card ♠-suit or was 4/4+ in majors
→ → 2♥	Advancer prefers ♥ (3+) or is neutral (2-2, 3-3), non-forcing
→ → → p	Overcaller had a weak 6-card ♥-suit or was 4/4+ in majors
→ → → 2♠	Overcaller had a weak 6-card ♠-suit

By preference. I mean a 3-card suit. Note that in some sequences we may end up in a Moysian 4-3 fit but often it will be a 6-3 fit. Opponents will be equally in the dark.

With only 2-2 in the majors, advancer gives ♥-preference. So occasionally we may even end up in a 4-2 ♥-suit when a 5-2 ♠-suit was available although this never happened to me in practice. With only 2-1 in the majors, advancer has ways of showing tolerance for a 2-card major with 5/5+ in minors which we will see shortly. I mention these drawbacks upfront but it would be unlucky indeed if advancer was not dealt even a 3-card major.

If a ♠-fit emerges, advancer has room for an invite to game:

(1N)-2♣-2♦-2♠   Mutual ♠-interest emerges

→ → → → 3♠   Advancer's general invite for game

→ → → → 3♣/3♦/3♥   Advancer's long-suit game-try

But advancer will not get a chance to explore over a ♥-fit (he does
not get another bid if overcaller passes, i.e. 2♣-2♥-P). So, if advancer
had interest in game contingent only on the overcaller having a ♥-
suit, then imagination is called for:

(1N)-2♣- 2♠   Pass or correct to 3♥; may continue if ♥-fit comes to light

Occasionally advancer will have a generally adaptable useful hand.
If he sees potential (or is just not willing to risk a 2♥-reply to be
passed out) then he should invoke an immediate 2NT enquiry. Then
overcaller can reply similarly as in her original overcall options over
the opponent's 1NT but now one level higher and at the same time
define her points range better. So, something along the following
lines:

(1N)-2♣-2N   Advancer's strong all-purpose general enquiry

→ → → 3♣   6-8 HCP, one or both majors

→ → → → 3♦   Advancer prefers ♠

→ → → → 3♥   Advancer prefers ♥

→ → → 3♦   9-10 HCP, both majors, 4/4+

→ → → 3M   9-10 HCP, 6-card major

10.4   Strong overcall hands

I said earlier that the 2♣ overcall with one or both majors can have
a strong hand variant. By strong I mean a 16+ HCP hand. This will
not happen very often especially over a strong 1NT but it is known to
happen when opponents play a weak 1NT. Even when it does come
up it will often be best for the overcaller to start with a double and
she may be able to come-in again following the opponents' probable
escape.

Nevertheless there are other strong major-suit hands which may be
unsuitable to double with. for instance such as where the major itself
is not a particularly good suit to lead from or where a double would
not be an adequate penalty due to relative vulnerability.

In those cases our overcaller can start with a 2♣ bid over their 1NT
and. whatever partner initially replies. rebid strongly to get across
the message. as follows:

(1N)-2♣	One major (6 cards) or both (4/4+). either 6-10 or 16+ HCP
→ → 2♦/♥	Advancer prefers ♠/♥. non-forcing
→ → → 3M	Overcaller reveals the 16+ HCP overcall hand. 6-card major
→ → → 2N	16+ HCP. both majors. 4/4+. not suitable for double first

All the above suit-rebids by the overcaller will be jump rebids except
in the sequence (1N)-2♣-2♥-3♥.

The overcaller's rebid is not forcing and partner can assume 16-18
HCP in judging whether to pass or bid a game. With an even bigger

hand overcaller may have even jumped to game with her rebid, if
not starting with a double in the first place.

10.5   If second opponent intervenes over our 2♣ overcall

If the second opponent (responder to their opener) bids over our
2♣ overcall then our partner (advancer to our overcaller) will often
pass on the assumption that our overcaller has a weak single-major
hand type. So will the overcaller unless she can come in again cheaply
at the 2-level with her weak 6-card major hand type.

There is still some room for improvisation by our advancer in some
situations. If the second opponent intervenes with a natural bid
(or a transfer ignoring our 2♣) and if the natural intervention (or
their anchor suit in case of a transfer) is a major then it is fair for
our advancer to assume that our overcaller probably had the other
major. So with a 3-card fit and some values our advancer should
come in at 2-level if that is available.

It is important to be on the same wavelength in these situations.
Our advancer assumes that our overcaller has the weak 6-card major
hand type and our overcaller assumes that advancer acts on that
basis showing a 3-card fit with fairly modest values. We had already
committed to play at the 2-level with no more than a 4-3 fit on a
bad day in the first place but fairly often we will be on a 6-3 fit with
which we should be competing.

We have so far assumed that the fact of the second opponent coming
into the bidding means that they are strong and we are weak and that

our overcaller had the weak 6-card major hand. But our advancer should be alert to the possibility that the second opponent came in, not out of strength, but out of weakness. If the opponents are playing Lebensohl-type methods then their sequence will also reveal their responder's worth.

If our overcaller had the stronger hand type then she will of course either double or continue bidding on her part when the bidding comes around to her again anyway.

If the second opponent/responder doubles our 2♣ overcall, whatever the double may mean, our advancer gains the option of passing. But we may as well give this pass a little more specific meaning by defining those hand types.

In practice I have found that it works best if our advancer only comes in over their double to bid 2♦/♥ when he has a 2-card or better differential preference between his own major suits lengths. So, passing instead specifically denies such strong preference between majors.

If the double reaches our overcaller then she can simply redefine her original overcall:

(1N)-2♣-(x)-p-(p)	Advancer denying a 2-card differential in majors
→ → → → → 2M	Overcaller owns up to her weak 6-card major
→ → → → → 2♦	Overcaller was weak 4-4 in majors, advancer to pick
→ → → → → xx	Overcaller was weak 5-4 in majors, either way
→ → → → → → 2♦	Advancer equal-length, overcaller to name 5-carder

But if the responding-opponent passes. our advancer bids 2♦ or 2♥ and then the opening-opponent doubles. (1N)-2♣-(p)-2♦-(x). this time some information has already been provided by our advancer and here our overcaller can complete our sequence.

10.6   Dealing with misfits

Although our 2♣ overcall is a 6-way bid. all those possibilities have a major-suit flavour. So if our advancer cannot stand either major (less than a doubleton in either major) and is himself weak with only minor-suit preponderance then he may have to improvise:

(1N)-2♣-p	Advancer weak with 6/7 clubs and no 2-card major
→ → 3♦	Advancer weak with 6/7 diamonds and no 2-card major
→ → 3♣	Advancer weak, 6/5+ minors, no 2-card M, pass or correct

If advancer dislikes hearts and only has spades. or has 2-card spade tolerance with one or both minors. then it is still best to start showing a ♠-preference and improvise later:

(1N)-2♣-2♦-2♥-2♠	Advancer weak with 6 spades, 0-1 hearts
→ → → → 2N	Advancer had 2-card ♠-suit and 5/5 minors, pick one
→ → → → 3m	Advancer had 2-card ♠-suit with 6-card minor as shown

Similarly if advancer dislikes spades and only has hearts. or has 2-card heart tolerance with one or both minors. then it is best to show ♥-preference first and then the rest of it:

(1N)-2♣-2♥-2♠-2N	Advancer had 2-card ♥-suit and 5/5 minors, pick one
→ → → → 3m	Advancer had 2-card ♥-suit with 6-card minor as shown
→ → → → 3♥	Advancer weak, 6/7 hearts, 0-1 spades, not-invitational

By contrast, initial jump replies by advancer in a major are best used to show an invitational single-major hand of his own and no tolerance for the other major, as if to say "I don't know which major you have but raise mine if you can or just pass":

(1N)-2♣-3M	Advancer invitational one-suited in major, 0-1 cards in other

10.7   Our other overcalls

For completeness let's also spell out our other possible overcalls over opponents' 1NT:

(1N)-x	Seeking penalty, 15-18 HCP
(1N)-2NT	5-5+ in minors with 11-15 HCP, OR any 2-suiter with 16+ HCP
(1N)-3any	Pre-emptive 6+ card suit

Please note that (1NT)-2NT may turn out to be any 2-suiter, 16+ HCP. 5/5+ shape. Advancer initially assumes the 2NT overcall to be 5/5+ in the minors with 11-15 HCP and shows preference on that basis. With the stronger alternative of any 2-suiter of 16+HCP our overcaller simply bids again in the cheaper of her two suits.

10.8   Passed hand overcalls

The system is not appropriate for a passed hand. We would have taken some action with probably all these hands in the opening position in the first place (the only possible exception being the 11-HCP 5-card major hands without a 4-card second suit alongside which might have therefore fallen outside the Rule of 20 to open a hand with).

Our passed-hand overcall structure therefore naturally presents itself as follows:

(1N)-2m   6-card natural minor-suit, 8-10 HCP

(1N)-2M   5-card natural major-suit, 8-10 (11) HCP

(1N)-x   Majors, 5/4 shape expected, 8-10 HCP

→ → 2♦   Advancer denies 2-card differential in majors, overcaller to pick

10.9   Other considerations

When playing a system which opponents will not have come across before, it is customary to offer them a suggested defence. The following seems appropriate:

- Following (1N)-2♣, opponents are advised to play 'systems on' and double for Stayman

- Following (1N)-2♦/♥/♠, opponents are advised to play 'systems on' e.g. Lebensohl

The other issue is that of disclosure on the convention card. Because the system does not have a name (but of course you are welcome to call them Kaban overcalls - thanks!). I suggest that you enter as much information as space will allow under the section 'defence against 1NT'. the following being a minimum disclosure:

(1N)-2♣   M or MM. weak or strong (replies: 2♦ = ♠. 2N = enquiry)

(1N)-2♦   MM. intermediate

Fuller description is recommended in your supplementary notes to your convention card.

Chapter 11

Weak-2 And Multi Sequences

11.1   Multi-2♦

Multi-2♦ is a wonderful system. For the sacrifice of a weak-2 opening bid in diamonds. or whatever it means in your system. it enables a gateway to a multiplicity of alternatives. I like my multi-2♦ as a 3-way bid. as follows:

- A weak-2 opening bid in a major. 6-10 HCP and 6-card suit; OR

- 20-21 HCP. fairly balanced hand; OR

- 18-21 HCP. 4-4-4-1 hands with any singleton

Most of the time opener's hand will reveal itself to be a weak-2 in a major.

Responder presumes that opener has a weak-2 in a major and so replies with most hands on a 'pass or correct' basis. It is important to bid immediately at the highest level of fit in responder's lesser major:

2♦*-2♥		0+ hearts and better spades (able to stand opener correcting to 2♠)
→	2♠	0+ spades and 3+ hearts (able to stand opener correcting to 3♥)
→	3♥	3 hearts and 3+ spades (able to stand opener correcting to 3♠)
→	3♠	3 spades and 4+ hearts (able to stand opener correcting to 4♥)

So, with a maximum 6-2 fit in either major responder will aim to keep to the 2-level but with 6-3 fit he is prepared to play at the 3-level and with a 6-4 fit at the 4-level, pretty much irrespective of combined high card points strength. So, responder continues with the pre-empting effort not only with intermediate hands but also with mutually weak hands, all of which makes it more difficult for the opponents to compete.

Opener ought to be in the better half of the 6-10 HCP range and hold a decent suit when opening in the 1st and 2nd positions (ahead of partner) but anything goes in the 3rd and 4th positions (with partner as a passed-hand).

The 3rd position is best not only for somewhat sub-standard weak-2 major openings especially when non-vulnerable but it is equally a good position to open some better hands at the 2-level, perhaps up to 12 HCP. The passed-hand partner is hardly going to get too excited to drive the bidding to game even if there is a good fit.

4th position equally lends itself to a wide-ranging weak-2 in a major but, realistically, you will never be holding a sub-standard weak-2 hand if all the other people at the table could not open the bidding. Therefore the 4th position weak-2 opener is more likely to be somewhat more intermediate than weak.

As a rule it would be right to alert a 3rd and 4th position multi-2♦ opening and explain that if it turns out to be a weak-2 in a major then the hand can be wider-ranging, perhaps 4-12 HCP rather than 6-10 HCP.

If responder is all-round strong enough to play at game-level in whatever major opener may hold, he can also choose who should play the hand. He can play the hand himself (perhaps to protect some delicate cards on the lead) or let opener play it:

2♦- 4♣   Asking opener to transfer to her major (so, responder plays it)

2♦- 4♦   Asking opener to bid her major (so, opener still plays it)

None of the above should be confused with an actual 4-major immediate response, which is no longer 'pass or correct' but is simply the contract responder wants to play:

2♦- 4♥/♠   To play, responder has a single-suited major hand of his own

Responder should not often diverge from a 'pass-or-correct' type of response but will sometimes have an unbalanced but strong hand himself or he may simply need to check opener's major and/or range before placing the final contract in opener's suit, in his own suit or even in no-trumps. With any such contingent responding hand types responder has the usual immediate 2NT response available as an Ogust-type enquiry:

2♦-2N			Responder's strong enquiry
→ → 3♣			6-8 HCP weak-2 in ♥
→ → → 3♦			Asking about top-3 ♥-honours (→ 3♥ = 0-1; 3♠ = 2 of top 3)
→ → 3♦			6-8 HCP weak-2 in ♠
→ → → 3♥			Asking about top-3 ♠-honours (→ 3♠ = 0-1; 3N = 2 of top 3)
→ → 3♥			9-10 HCP weak-2 in ♥
→ → 3♠			9-10 HCP weak-2 in ♠
→ → 3N			AKQxxx in a major
→ → 4any			18-21 HCP, 4-4-4-1 with singleton as shown

The Ogust reply structure has become inverted over the years so that minor suit replies nowadays normally show the better weak-2 hands but I prefer the original version because we can add to it a second round enquiry as in the above structure to check the top cards in opener's major in case they are still good enough to make a run for some game contract. Note that the bidding still does not exceed 3 of the relevant major suit even if opener delivers two negative replies to responder's enquiries.

So far we have concerned ourselves with only the weak-2 major variety of the multi-2♦ opening bids. There will of course be times when opener has the 20-21 HCP balanced hand type or the 18-21 HCP 4-4-4-1 (any singleton) hand type. That is how the sequences will unravel in those cases after responder initially assumes the weak-2 variety and makes his initial response on a 'pass-or-correct' basis:

2♦-2M	Pass or correct
→ → 2N	Opener reveals 20-21 HCP hand type; OR
→ → 3any	18-21 HCP, 4441 with singleton shown (but 2♦-2♠-3N=single-♥)

The sequence 2♦-2♠-3N shows a ♥-singleton because 2♦-2♠-3♥ must remain as opener's correction to a weak-2 in hearts.

If the 'pass-or-correct' response was at the 3-level then we have:

2♦-3M	Pass or correct, with 3+ cards in both majors
→ → 3N	Opener had 20-21 hand type (or 18-21 HCP any 4-4-4-1 hand)
→ → 4M	Opener had 20-21 hand type with a 5-card fit for the major

After a 2♦-3M start the 18-21 HCP 4-4-4-1 hand types are also squeezed into the 3NT response because we do not want to bypass 3NT as a possible final contract and also we want to use the 4-level to locate any 4-4 major suit fits which we may still have. So:

2♦-3M-3N-4♣	4-card Stayman enquiry
→ → → → 4♦	No 4-card majors
→ → → → → 4N	To play (Not RKCB)

When partner more specifically reveals the 20-21 HCP balanced hand type at the 2-level (namely, the sequence 2♦-2M-2NT) then a whole series of possibilities arise. We will cover these on page 147 in Strong-2 Sequences.

We will also return to the 4-4-4-1 hands on page 153 in Strong-2 Sequences, to recap not just those in the 18-21 HCP range but also stronger and weaker 4-4-4-1 hands.

Let's also deal with the situations where opponents intervene with our multi-2♦ sequences. The first thing to say is that we should keep to the same structure of responses as much as possible whether the first opponent doubles or overcalls our multi-2♦ opener. So, our pass-or-correct responses still apply and so does our 2NT enquiry, in effect ignoring the intervention. But an immediate 3NT response over any double or overcall is to play.

If our multi-2♦ opener is doubled we gain two extra bids, pass and redouble. Responder's pass should mean equal length in the majors (still continuing to assume that opener has a weak-2 in a major, our default assumption). But more than that, pass should mean 2-2 in the majors (or possibly 1-1) because with any 3-card major, let alone 3-cards in both majors, responder should be making the system's usual pass-or-correct bid.

Redouble is more interesting. It is redundant as a natural bid and so I suggest it should show willingness to play at the 3-level in spades only (but not in hearts), which is the only pass-or-correct reply for major suits that is not otherwise possible to show cheaply.

If the opponents overcall in any suit then our responder's double is always for penalties. The beauty of weak-2 opening bids including those via the multi-2♦ opener is that they describe opener's hand so well in one go that responder is able to decide to take a penalty if the opportunity arises with opponents guessing wrong as they try to enter the bidding at potentially an uncomfortable level for them.

If our opener has one of the stronger hand types for her multi-2♦ opening then of course she will herself want to take some action against any indiscretion by opponents that may come round to her. I suggest the following:

- Opener's re-opening double or redouble = 20-21 HCP, fairly balanced

- Opener's re-opening 2NT rebid = 18-21 HCP, 3-suited 4-4-4-1 hands

The above are akin to my suggested re-opening action by a 2♣ opener and I will cover them more comprehensively on page 146 in Strong-2 Sequences. including the rationale of a 2NT rebid to show more than one place to play but not promising a stopper in any opponent suit.

11.2   Muiderberg 2♥ and 2♠

With the multi-2♦ taking care of our weak-2 bids with a 6-card major. the opening bids of 2♥ and 2♠ are available for something a little different.

Two-suited weak hands are my choice here.   To increase the frequency. I prefer these to denote specifically 5-cards in the major that is being shown together with a minor suit of 4 cards or longer. all still in a weak hand in the 6-10 HCP range.

5-5 shape is possible but not a requirement for Muiderberg 2M opening bids (5-5 shape requirement would make it the Lucas convention).   Also. if a 6th card is held in the major we use multi-2♦ instead to concentrate on that 6-card holding even if we have a 4-card or longer minor alongside.

The second suit should not be the other major; holding both majors I would not normally want to give up on the possibility of a fit in my shorter major even if that is a 4-card suit. So I would rarely pre-empt holding 6-4, 5-4 or 5-5 in the majors.

Following a Muiderberg 2M, if responder cannot stand the major he can try the minor:

2M	6-10 HCP, 5 card Major as bid and a 4+ card minor
→ 3♣	Pass or correct to other minor, not forward-going

But if responder has a good hand with some potential he can invoke a 2NT enquiry:

2M-2N	Enquiry
→ → 3m	Lower range, 6-8 HCP, with the minor shown
→ → 3♥	Upper range, 9-10 HCP, with ♣
→ → 3♠	Upper range, 9-10 HCP, with ♦

If responder already has a fit for the major and a game-going hand, there is a tool to explore the best contract and even investigate slam possibilities:

2M-3♦	Artificial game-force, partner's major agreed as trumps
→ → 3M	Opener's rebid of her major promises a void somewhere
→ → 3other	A new suit by opener shows a singleton there
→ → 3NT	2-2 shape alongside 5-card Major and 4-card minor

To ask opener to identify her void after a start of. say. 2♥-3♦-3♥. responder bids the next step. here 3♠. In reply. 4♣ or 4♦ shows a void there. A rebid of the agreed major (4♥) is the 'impossible void' which serves to show a higher ranking suit. so a ♠-void. This neat proxy bidding as an impossible reply is necessary because we do not want to take the bidding beyond 4♥ in case the revelation of the void suit does not particularly help.

Similarly. after the alternative start of 2♠-3♦-3♠. the asking next step is 3NT. Opener's 4♣. 4♦ and 4♥ replies name her void suit. 3NT can not be a natural bid here because. having earlier agreed opener's major and now being made aware of a void. responder would not be offering 3NT as a possible final contract.

Let's also deal with the situations where opponents intervene with our Muiderberg sequences. As with our multi-2♦ sequences. we keep to the same responses as much as possible whether the first opponent doubles or overcalls our 2♥ or 2♠ opener. So. our pass-or-correct responses still apply and so does our 2NT enquiry. in effect ignoring the intervention. But an immediate 3NT response over any double or overcall is to play.

If our Muiderberg 2M opener is doubled then responder's pass shows 2+ cards in the major and no better place to go.

Responder's redouble would be an SOS call. It shows a single-suited hand. 6+ cards in a good suit of his own to bail out to. Opener bids the next suit up as a pass-or-correct relay and responder signs off in his intended suit. which could be 2♠ after an initial 2♥ opening but more likely will be a level higher in 3♣ or 3♦.

If the opponents overcall in a suit then our responder's double is always for penalties. Like the multi-2♦ openers, Muiderberg 2♥ and 2♠ openers are also very descriptive and limited opening bids so that responder can decide to take a penalty if the opponents guess their overcalls wrong over our opening bids.

11.3   Unusual 2NT opening bid

As the strong balanced hand is covered plentifully through 2♦-multi and 2♣ openers, the 2NT opening bid is available for something more exotic, such as a weak 2-suiter, either majors or minors, at least 5-5 or longer. This also completes the range of weak 2-suited combinations if our 2M openers are of the Muiderberg (or Lucas) variety.

You no doubt use 2NT jump overcalls as weak two-suited bids, so why not also use 2NT opening bids similarly as weak two-suited bids.

Here's a very playable 2NT opening bid and response structure:

2NT	6-10 HCP, either majors or minors, 5/5+
→ 3m	Responder's better minor, to play if opener has mm
→ 3♥	Strong enquiry (→ opener bids 3♠ with MM, 3NT with mm)
→ 3♠/4m/4M	To pass or correct to the cheaper of the right 2-suits
→ 3NT	To play

6-10 HCP is a fair range but the hand should be capable of buying the contract because the information given away does not fare well in defence. Committing to the 3-level also means that 2NT openers should not be very weak when vulnerable.

A case could be made for a partnership understanding that all 10-counts even with both majors should be opened 2NT, rather than opening 1M under the Rule of 20, so that all 1M openings become at worst a reliable 11-HCP with shape given that responder will often be committing the partnership to game on a 12-count under the 2/1 system.

All non-forcing responder hands will start with the better minor, 3♣ being the default choice. If opener reveals that he had the majors by continuing to 3♥ then responder will pass that or correct to 3♠. It doesn't cost responder to start with an initial 3♣ response even if he is fairly sure that opener must have the majors; indeed he should especially start with 3♣ if he has game potential contingent on finding opener with both majors, so that he gets another bid in the event that opener corrects 3♣ to 3♥.

Whenever responder holds one major and one minor he knows that there will be a fit somewhere. All suit bids from 3♠ to 4♠ are non-forcing pass-or-correct bids. If having to correct, opener simply bids the cheaper of the appropriate pair of suits.

When responder has the values or shape to force to game then he starts with an artificial 3♥ enquiry to clarify whether opener had the majors (3♠) or the minors (3NT). Responder then decides. Of course he may have had his own agenda all along, such as a long suit of his own to play game in, the 3♥ being an all-purpose force.

So, 2NT-3♥-3NT-4♠ shows that responder had a very good 6+ card spade suit and a game-force all along, whereas a direct 2NT-4♠ would allow opener to correct to a minor at the 5-level if he had minors. 2NT-3♠ is a more limited non-forcing response with spades and a minor.

The initial 3♥ game-forcing relay could also include any slam-try hand. 3NT-3♥-3NT-4m. for example. is not just choosing a minor suit but must also be MSRKCB in that minor suit given that we were already in a game-force sequence after the initial 3♥.

2NT-3NT is to play although this is almost a redundant sequence since responder could equally go via 3♥ at no cost and occasionally discover a surprise big fit. (The more adventurous may even consider giving other meanings to the 3NT-raise. perhaps a slam-try if opener has both majors). In the absence of any alternative meaning the 3NT-raise should remain a semi-balanced game-going hand presumably with a minor suit flavour because it is spurning the option of playing in a 5-3 major fit.

Majors-or-minors 2NT opening bids are difficult for the opponents to interfere with (as compared to the minors-only variety). If the first opponent tries a natural suit overcall this may even clarify the situation for our responder before the next opponent can come in.

If the first opponent doubles. it is best not to engage with the opponents about what it means but simply assume that it was an improvised attempt to show general values.

When opponents overcall or double my unusual 2NT opening bid. I have a good menu of continuations including some fine-tuning:

- Response system remains ON as before, plus the following refinements:

- Responder's doubles of opponents' overcalls are for penalties

- 2NT-(x)-p = responder has no 3-card minor

- 2NT-(x)-xx = responder's has own 6+ suit (→ 3♣ as pass-or-correct)

- After 2NT-(p/x)-3♣-(p), opener's 3♦ = good-MM, 3♥ = poor-MM

- After 2NT-(p/x)-3♣-(x), opener's pass = mm, 3♦=good-MM, 3♥=poor-MM

- After 2NT-(p/x)-3♥*-(x), opener's pass=MM, 3♠=good-mm, 3N=poor-mm

Beware that the minors-or-majors 2NT opening bid may be a disallowed convention at some levels in some jurisdictions because it is a 2-level bid without any specific anchor suit. For example in England it is not allowed in Level 3 events which generally cover club level bridge but it is fine at Level 4 which covers most county and nearly all national events. You should switch to a simpler minors-only version when the minors-or-majors variety is not permitted.

The more adventurous of you may also like to consider playing the 2NT opening bid not only as majors-or-minors but also as weak-or-strong. More fun is guaranteed!

Chapter 12

Strong-2 Sequences

12.1   Strong 2♣ and Kokish-style responses

I use the 2♣ opening bid as a game-force for both balanced hands and suit-based hands. The balanced and semi-balanced hands promise 22+ HCP. My suit-based hands could be a single-suited, two-suited or three-suited hand promising a game-level trick-taking capacity assuming reasonable distribution of our key suit(s) among the other three hands.

The only rebid that responder is allowed to pass out below game is the sequence 2♣-2♦-2NT which shows 22-23 HCP. Otherwise responder must co-operate to game-level.

All responses start with a 2♦-relay giving opener the floor again to describe her hand type better. Often a second 2-level relay is involved before opener's hand is more particularly defined within the said hand type. For these reasons responder does not attempt to describe his own hand at all initially but waits until opener finishes.

My preferred Kokish-style structure begins to unravel opener's hand as follows:

2♣			22+ HCP balanced or strong 1/2/3-suited hand
→	2♦		Relay
→	→	2♥	Artificial - usually 2-suited hand (see below for continuations)
→	→	2♠	Artificial - any 3-suited GF hand (see below for continuations)
→	→	2N	22-23 HCP balanced or semi-balanced (see next section)
→	→	3♣	Single-suited ♣ game-force
→	→	3♦	Single-suited ♦ game-force
→	→	3♥	Single-suited ♥ game-force
→	→	3♠	Single-suited ♠ game-force
→	→	3N	26+ HCP balanced or semi-balanced (see next section)

So. after 2♣-2♦ all opener 3-level rebids are single-suited game-force in the said suit whereas the 2NT and 3NT rebids are balanced hands of different strength.

2-suited strong opener hands need a second relay:

2♣-2♦-2♥	Artificial, seeking further relay
→ → → 2♠	Relay
→ → → → 2N	24-25 HCP balanced or semi-balanced
→ → → → 3♣	2-suited, ♣ and a Major
→ → → → → 3♦	Identify your major
→ → → → → other	Cue-bid, with ♣ set as trumps
→ → → → 3♦	2-suited, ♦ and ♥
→ → → → → 3♥	Sets ♥
→ → → → → other	Cue-bid, with ♦ set as trumps
→ → → → 3♥	2-suited, ♥ and ♠
→ → → → → 3♠	Sets ♠
→ → → → → other	Cue-bid, with ♥ as trumps
→ → → → 3♠	2-suited, ♠ and ♦
→ → → → → 4♦	Sets ♦
→ → → → → other	Cue-bid, with ♠ as trumps
→ → → → 3N	2-suited, minors
→ → → → → 4m	Responder's better minor

And the 3-suited varieties are spelt out as follows:

2♣-2♦-2♠	Artificial, 3-suited, 22+ HCP, any 4-4-4-1 or 5-4-4-0
→ → → 2N	Relay
→ → → → 3♣	3-suited hand with singleton or void ♣
→ → → → 3♦	3-suited hand with singleton or void ♦
→ → → → 3♥	3-suited hand with singleton or void ♥
→ → → → 3♠	3-suited hand with singleton or void ♠

After opener completes describing her hand responder normally assumes control with a view to assessing prospects and judging the ultimate contract.

If opponents intervene with our 2♣ sequences we need clear methods to deal with them. An element of improvisation and common sense is indispensible but some general principles are essential, perhaps along the following lines:

- Opener's re-opening double or redouble = 22+ HCP, fairly balanced

- Opener's re-opening 2NT rebid = 2-suited or even 3-suited hand

- Opener's re-opening suit-rebid = natural one suited or not-balanced

- Responder's free bid over intervening double or bid is natural with values

A re-opening double of an overcall is easier to associate with a generally rounded big hand and it has more frequency than a strictly negative double (which would necessarily have had to imply shortage in opponent's intervention suit). The same criteria also goes for re-doubling LHO's double of your own 2♣ or the RHO's double of partner's 2♦-relay.

If that's what a double more meaningfully covers then that leaves the 2NT rebid now to show 2 places to play if not 3 places. With only a single-suited hand for your original 2♣ opening bid then you would of course want to show your suit with your rebid anyway.

The above use of the 2NT rebid has more frequency than using it to show the big hand type with stoppers in their intervention suit. That way you would often be torn between showing the stopper and showing the real features of your hand. Note that our 2NT rebid, not being a natural bid, does not promise a stopper in any suit the opponents may have overcalled in.

12.2   Strong balanced hands

Let's pull together the various strong balanced hand types I have talked about in different sections so far, above the 15-17 HCP 1NT opening bid strength:

18-19 HCP	1x-1y-2NT; or 1y-2x-2NT as dual range 12-14 or 18-19 HCP
20-21 HCP	2♦-2M-2NT; or 2♦-3M-3NT; or 2♦-3M-4M (5-card raise)
22-23 HCP	2♣-2♦-2NT
24-25 HCP	2♣-2♦-2♥-2♠-2NT
26+ HCP	2♣-2♦-3NT

I strongly favour 2-point ranges for the strong balanced hands. This makes it much easier for both opener and responder with subsequent quantitative raise decisions.

Let's also remember that these hands may not be perfectly balanced. In practice they may include some atypical shapes, including a singleton Ace (or even the King) if for example the hand-pattern is any 1-3-4-5 or even 1-3-3-6 with a 6-card minor. This may be necessary when you cannot risk partner passing out your 1-level opening bid.

By way of continuation by responder, over the 18-19 HCP rebid we have the New Minor Forcing ('NMF') convention available. So 3♣ by responder asks about major suits features, unless opener had opened

1♣ in which case responder's asking bid would be 3♦. We will cover NMF more specifically on page 199 in Fine-tuning.

With all other strong balanced hand types we have the following continuation structure:

2N	20-21 via 2♦, 22-23 via 2♣-2♦-2N, 24-25 via 2♣-2♦-2♥-2♠-2N, etc
→ 3♣	5-card Puppet Stayman (see next section)
→ 3♦	Transfer to ♥
→ 3♥	Transfer to ♠
→ 3♠	Slam-try in either minor, promising 5/4+ cards in minors
→ 3N	To play (probably without a 3-card major)
→ 4N	Quantitative (probably without a 3-card major)

3♠ slam-try in either minor is useful especially if requiring only a 5/4+ shape, but it needs good communications thereafter. I favour the following method:

2N-3♠	Slam-suitable hand in both minor suits, promising 5/4+
→ → 4m	Opener choosing 4+ card minor suit but not keen on slam
→ → 4♥	Opener interested, step-RKCB for ♣
→ → 4♠	Opener interested, step-RKCB for ♦

By step-RKCB, I mean Roman Key Card Blackwood but with responses in individual steps, showing 0, 1, 2, 3, 4, 5 key cards, one at a time (i.e. non-composite answers). This may be followed by a trump-Queen enquiry and/or side-Kings enquiry on the same principles. We will discuss some different versions of RKCB in different situations in Chapter 13.

How about 4-level jump-responses to 2NT? I like those as 'two-under' slam-try bids for a 6+ card single-suited responder-hand, as follows:

2N-4♣   Slam-try in ♥ (→ 4♦= co-operative; 4♥= sign-off; 4NT = RKCB in ♥)

→ 4♦   Slam-try in ♠ (→ 4♥= co-operative; 4♠= sign-off; 4NT = RKCB in ♠)

→ 4♥   Slam-try in ♣ (→ 4♠= co-operative; 4NT = to play; 5♣ = sign-off)

→ 4♠   Slam-try in ♦ (→ 4NT = to play; 5♣ = co-operative; 5♦ = sign-off)

You will have spotted the pattern with the 'two-under' replies and further continuations. Responder shows interest in slam by bidding the suit that is two suits below his slam suggestion suit. This beginning enables opener a short-break reply option into the in-between suit as a co-operative move.

This also means that opener can give a lesser reply by bidding an immediate sign-off in the intended suit, a kind of 'fast-arrival' reply. If a major this would probably be a doubleton. But the structure also enables opener to super-accept a major by starting RKCB herself.

With minors, however, a 4NT reply by opener is better played as a natural bid, offering this as a final resting place. This is especially useful in matchpoints, with no fit for the suggested minor suit but stops elsewhere.

Finally, it is customary to play the same 2NT continuations structure as a whole also after we overcall opponents' weak-2 or multi-2♦ openings with a 2NT showing 16-18 HCP. This may be closer to our 1NT-range than our 2NT-ranges but we do not have much choice anymore once the opponents' pre-emptive bid takes a level of bidding away and forces us to start at the 2NT-level to show any kind of balanced hand. Using the same methods after this 2NT at least provides consistency with all our other 2NT-systems, including the 3♣ Puppet Stayman continuations to which we turn next.

12.3 2NT-3♣ Puppet Stayman sequences

Much of the rationale that we discussed in Chapter 8 about 1NT-2♣ Puppet Stayman methods apply equally to 2NT-3♣ Puppet Stayman sequences.

However, there are also some differences. For one thing we have less space over 2NT. There is therefore no room for invitational bids after asking about majors or transferring to a major. The fact that our 2NT bids comprise 2-point ranges helps a little here.

The other difference with Puppet over 2NT is that opener may have some off-shapes including not only a 5-card major but even 5-4 in the majors. Or, indeed, responder may have 5-4 in the majors himself. All this needs to be unscrambled in relatively limited bidding space.

A useful additional tool to deal with some of these hand shapes is to allow opener to show a 3-card spade suit when she has one. So, opener's first reply to the Puppet enquiry now shows whether she holds a major which could include a 3-card spade suit or she has nothing at all in majors:

2N-3♣	5-card Puppet Stayman
→ → 3N	Opener has neither 3+ spades nor 4+ hearts
→ → 3♦	Opener has at least one 4-card major or 3 spades

If responder has spades, or both majors, then we have:

2N-3♣-3♦- 3♥	Responder has 4 or 5 spades, may also have 4 hearts
→ → → → 3♠	Opener has 4 hearts, denies 4 spades
→ → → → 3N	Opener has 3 spades, denies 4 hearts
→ → → → 4♠	Opener has spade fit with responder

If responder had 4 spades and 5 hearts then rather than bidding Puppet he would have transferred to hearts and then bid spades. But with 5 spades and 4 hearts, in order to investigate a fit in either major, he needs to start with 3♣, just like he would have done with 4-4. If opener initially replies 3♦ (at least one 4-card major or 3-card spade suit) then responder still continues with 3♥ anchoring to spades, which opener at this stage assumes to be a 4-card suit. But once opener bids a third time, 3♠ or 3NT or 4♠, all is revealed and responder names the final contract (which may be 4♠ if he had 5 spades all along and opener shows 3 with 3NT).

The bidding is less complicated if responder has hearts alone:

2N-3♣-3♦- 3♠	Responder has 4 hearts, denies 4 spades
→ → → → 3N	Opener has 3 or 4 spades, denies 4 hearts
→ → → → 4♥	Opener has heart fit with responder

Even when responder does not have a 4-card major himself but only a 3-card suit, he still needs to start with 3♣ to check for a 5-card major fit in opener's hand. If opener replies 3♦ promising lesser major suit features then responder can abort:

2N-3♣-3♦- 3N   Responder had no 4 card major (was checking for 5)

→ → → 4N   Quantitative (having checked for any 5 card major first)

Of course some of the time opener will have a 5-card major, in which
case we have some very straightforward bidding:

2N-3♣- 3♥   Opener has 5 hearts

→ → 3♠   Opener has 5 spades

The more particular continuation 2NT-3♣-3♥-3♠ could be two
things. Firstly, it could be that responder was only looking for a
4-4 spade fit and, having heard of opener's 5-card heart suit, is now
further checking for a spade fit in case opener had an exact 4-5-2-2
shape.

Secondly, it could be a prelude to RKCB in hearts, the principle
being that 4NT by responder here is always quantitative (whether
opener shows or denies a major) and so, in order to set hearts as
trumps, responder travels via the other major, spades, before bidding
4NT now as RKCB for hearts.

This works because the other major is usually a redundant bid in
these sequences. Even a forgetful opener would at least continue the
bidding for the moment because the other major sounds forcing if
nothing else and she will no doubt remember it all when responder
next bids 4NT. So, we get:

2N-3♣-3♥-3♠-any-4N   becomes RKCB for hearts (cancelling the earlier 3♠)

2N-3♣-3♠-4♥-4♠-4N   becomes RKCB for spades (cancelling the earlier 1♥)

The above route therefore leaves all second-round 4NT rebids by responder as quantitative even after opener responds positively with a 5-card major:

2N-3♣-3♥-4N   Quantitative (responder must have been seeking spade-fit)

2N-3♣-3♠-4N   Quantitative (responder must have been seeking heart-fit)

2N-3♣-3♦-4N   Quantitative (having checked for any 5 card major first)

2N-3♣-3N-4N   Quantitative (having checked any major suit fit first)

If an opponent doubles our 3♣ Puppet enquiry perhaps as a lead-director then we can play the same system that I suggested upon their double of our 2♣ Puppet enquiry. Opener passes the double to show club-stop(s) and now responder redoubles to reconvene our sequence and in effect opener gets in two replies, first showing the club-stop and then giving the real answer to the 3♣ enquiry. By inference, an immediate reply to the 3♣ enquiry ignoring the double denies a club-stopper.

12.4   Strong 3-suited hands

I covered different 3-suited hand types and ranges in different sections. Let me now pull them all together here again.

With 22+ HCP and any 4-4-4-1 or 5-4-4-0 hand, we open 2♣:

2♣-2♦-2♠	Artificial, 3-suited, 22+ HCP, any 4-4-4-1 or 5-4-4-0
→ → → 2N	Second relay
→ → → → 3♣/♦/♥/♠	3-suited 22+ HCP hand with singleton or void as bid

With 18-21 HCP and any 4-4-4-1 hand (but not 5-4-4-0 hands) we start with 2♦:

2♦- 2M	Pass or correct to other major (assuming weak-2)
→ → 3♣/♦/♥/♠	18-21 HCP, 4441 with singleton shown (see exception)

So, 2♦-2♥-3♥ would be a ♥-singleton and 2♦-2♠-3♠ a ♠-singleton in an 18-21 HCP hand (surely the weak-2 opener is not entitled to a natural raise). Please note that 2♦-2♥-3♠ (jump) shows the ♠-singleton because 2♦-2♥-2♠ would have been opener's correction to spades. By way of exception 2♦-2♠-3NT shows a ♥-singleton because 2♦-2♠-3♥ would have been opener's correction to hearts. So, opener always rebids at the 3-level even if it is a jump or seems like 'raising' responder, the only systematic exception being the 2♦-2♠-3NT sequence which, by elimination, also makes sense.

If the initial 'pass-or-correct' response was at the 3-level then we cannot do everything:

2♦- 3M	Pass or correct, with 3+ cards in both majors
→ → 3N	18-21 HCP any 4-4-4-1 hand OR 20-21 HCP balanced

After a 2♦-3M start the 18-21 HCP 4-4-4-1 hand types as well as the 20-21 HCP balanced hand types are squeezed into the 3NT response because we do not want to bypass 3NT as a possible final contract.

There is no room to particularly investigate the singleton in this situation but that does not necessarily spell disaster. It is also the case that we will want to use the 4-level to locate any 4-4 major suit fit which we may still have.

Responder would typically continue with 2♦-3M-3NT-4♣ as a 4-card Stayman enquiry in this instance. If this locates a 4-4 major suit fit, all is well. But if the enquiry does not reveal a fit, or if opener responds 4♦ denying a 4-card major, a subsequent 4NT by responder must be reserved as natural and final (not RKCB). If opener does have a 4-4-4-1 hand, but no fit, then it is likely that opener's singleton is responder's main suit in which case a no-trumps contract is probably the logical resting place.

The 3-suited hands in the 18-21 HCP range via 2♦ comprise 4-4-4-1 hands alone and so exclude 5-4-4-0 hands. That is because with 5-4-4-0 hands and 18+ HCP you can afford to open at the 1-level in your 5-card suit and if partner responses in one of your suits then make a splinter rebid in your void but if partner responses in no-trumps or in your void suit then reverse or jump-shift into your 4-card suit.

The above better route for dealing with those hands means that the 2♦-route is specifically a singleton-bearing 3-suited hand, never a void. This differentiation can provide additional clarification to the continuations once a 3-suited hand type is confirmed after a 2♦-start.

Finally, what about 4-4-4-1 hands with 17 HCP? Well, if the singleton is a minor suit Ace or King, I don't mind opening the hand as 1NT. This is not as dangerous as it sounds. If partner has a major suit feature he will no doubt investigate a fit there and all will be well. If on the other hand partner does not investigate a major suit fit this is often a sign that he has minor suit features and will often prefer to play in no-trumps anyway. It is of course possible that he may seek a minor suit transfer but then he will also get to hear your misfit when you short-break the transfer and sometimes he will also be passing that.

I wouldn't suggest a 1NT opening bid with a major suit singleton Ace or King because we have too many sequences with which partner needs to be relying on at least two cards support in your lesser major.

Chapter 13

Blackwood Collection

Of course everyone plays Blackwood. That goes without saying. But are you making the most of it? Do you play any special sequences or variants of Blackwood? Can you deal with a void in either hand? Can you speculatively investigate a minor suit slam but still retain the option to sign off at a safe-level - even in 4NT for a better matchpoints result.

We will come to my version of minor-suit RKCB later. First, here's a recap of some everyday Roman Key Cay Blackwood stuff, most of which you probably already know.

Some of the tools below are appropriate within regular RKCB and some others are intended only for other variations of RKCB. The distinction will become clear as you go through them and I also provide a RKCB matrix later in this section, on page 167.

13.1   Either/or   responses   to   side-Kings enquiry

As we know. following the initial 4NT RKCB enquiry and partner's response. and sometimes also after checking the trump suit Queen if that was an issue. a 5NT follow-on bid confirms that all five key cards (four Aces and the trump suit King) are present and at the same asks about the three side suit Kings.

In reply. traditionally some people give the number of side Kings held whereas others like to name them upwards. Both are imperfect methods. Partner may need to know whether a specific side King is held. The total number held is not going to help unless that means all happen to be held between the two hands and naming them upwards is not going to work if the critical King is in a higher ranking suit than the trump suit which you may not want to risk going beyond.

Instead. replying on an 'either/or' basis deals with this problem. That is. any side suit you reply in shows either that side King alone or not that one but the other two instead. So if hearts are trumps and the 5NT enquiry fetches a 6♣ response then that shows either the ♣-King alone or both the ♦-King and ♠-King.

The answer on an either/or basis reveals both the number and suit(s) of the side Kings held by partner. What's more. if any side King is still missing. you can now work it out specifically. Neither opponent (unless holding a King) will share the same information.

Discipline requires that you need to hold one side King of your own (or be prepared to play in 6NT) in case partner's reply carries the bidding beyond 6 of the intended trump suit. It is not too much to ask that you hold a side-King yourself before you embark on a 5NT enquiry.

13.2 Either/or responses to trump-Queen enquiry

We can apply the same principles when replying favourably to any trump-Queen enquiry. But first let's go back a step or two in our RKCB sequence.

Obviously some of the time the initial 4NT RKCB enquiry will find partner with two key cards in which case his response at the same time will also either confirm the trump-Queen (5♠) or deny it (5♥). But if partner has a key card count other than two then the initial response of 5♣ or 5♦ will not have dealt with the trump-Queen issue either way.

Incidentally I hope that you play 41/30 responses to the initial 4NT RKCB enquiry. The bigger hand tends to do the asking in RKCB sequences and when partner also has some values but not specifically two key cards then the chances of him having one key card is greater than having none. In those cases a 5♣ reply, compared to a 5♦ reply, leaves an extra step for a follow-on trump-Queen enquiry. The difference translates to being able to carry out a cost-free follow-on Queen enquiry when the trumps are hearts.

When partner replies 5♣ or 5♦ and you don't have the trump-Queen yourself (or a 10-card trump fit) but have room to explore, then the next non-trump step of course asks about the missing trump-Queen. Partner signs off in the trump suit if he doesn't have the Queen and I like to use a 5NT reply to show the trump-Queen but no side-Kings.

When partner does have the trump-Queen and one or more side-Kings, how about using the same either/or method that we discussed earlier about side Kings? Perfect!

So when partner replies in a side suit to your trump-Queen enquiry, this confirms not only the trump-Queen but also either the side King of the named suit or the other two. Provided you have a side King of your own you again know everything there is to know.

13.3 When responder has a void

When you have a void, you would normally prefer to do your slam exploration through cue bidding. But sometimes partner starts a 4NT RKCB sequence of his own accord.

No matter. There are exceptional replies you can give to the 4NT enquiry, as follows:

5NT	2 key cards plus a void (not in partner's 1st suit)
6 of a suit below trumps	1 or 3 key cards plus void in the named suit
6 trumps	1 or 3 key cards plus void in a higher-ranking suit

It is so simple and yet so effective. The pleasure of being able to communicate a higher-ranking void by jumping to slam in our trump suit in response to partner's 4NT enquiry is immeasurable. When this came up at the table my only problem was whether I should be alerting it for the benefit of the opponents (which I did and my explanation was met with predictable surprise by the opponents but later they duly acknowledged the precision).

Responder does not attempt to show a void if he has no key cards at all.

13.4 When enquirer has a void (Exclusion-RKCB)

Not only can you reply to show a void as responder but you can also start a RKCB enquiry by showing a void on your part as the enquirer.

The Exclusion-RKCB, or Voidwood as it is also known, is in practice a triple-jump (a level higher than a splinter) in a suit which shows a void in that suit and at the same starts a RKCB enquiry excluding that suit.

The exclusion-suit can be an unbid suit or the opponents' suit but not partner's suit. If it happens before specific suit agreement then the last naturally bid suit by you or partner is presumed set as the trump suit.

Taking out the enquirer's void suit, the replies will be based on the three working Aces plus the trump-King, so now only four key cards in total. Partly because of the random starting point for Exclusion-

RKCB. I prefer my key card count replies to be in non-composite steps. so showing 0. 1. 2. 3 or 4 key cards counting one step at a time in reply including 4/5NT as steps.

The enquirer may follow with trump-Queen enquiry and/or side-Kings enquiry. which we will discuss specifically shortly.

When replying to Exclusion. responder does not try to show any void of his own.

13.5   Minor-suit RKCB ('MSRKCB')

This convention enables most minor suit slam possibilities to be investigated while keeping below the level of game. Basically, it treats forward-going bids of 4♣ and 4♦ as directly initiating a RKCB enquiry in the indicated minor. Before discussing the mechanics, it is perhaps worth highlighting the rationale and the main forms of its use.

In its original form this convention is intended for investigating minor suit hands with a pronounced distribution which, even if possibly underweight in terms of high-card points, may just play for slam with a complementing hand opposite. So, it is particularly useful at teams where the slam bonus is all important and it is best to go for the safest slam. At its crudest. a 4♣ or 4♦ rebid after a strong-2♣ opener initiates the MSRKCB convention. The 4m starting point provides room for some initial enquiries to be made but, if no favourable news is forthcoming. then still affords a safe sign-off at 5m.

Although not part of the original convention, it seems to me that it can also be used to good effect especially at matchpointed pairs in the somewhat different situation when a 3NT contract seems certain but there is also a possibility of a minor suit slam. The same convention can in fact allow a minor suit slam to be safely investigated below the 5-level, provided that an additional mechanism is added so that we can even sign-off in 4NT if we have to and still aim for a good matchpoints result in no-trumps.

When in the absence of a good initial response we can have two possible safe sign-off points, 4NT or 5m, then the prospects for speculative use of this version of MSRKCB is greatly enhanced. Indeed it would be a shame not to investigate a minor suit slam whenever we reach 3NT but feel we have values to spare with minor suit oriented hands.

The only proviso is that the 4♣ or 4♦ must be a clearly forward-going bid rather than a natural scramble or a safety bail-out. If it is ambiguous in intent, it must be treated as natural and non-forcing, in which case partner may pass it (or raise it to game). If you want to make a forcing bid of 4♣ or 4♦ but you are uncertain whether it will be read as forcing, then you must instead pick some other explicitly forcing bid or revert to using the ordinary 4NT RKCB enquiry in the first place. Please also note that when you play MSRKCB there is also no invitational minor suite raise to 4♣ or 4♦ anymore.

In responding to a 4m MSRKCB enquiry, I think that non-composite step replies work best, again partly because the enquiry can have two different starting points (4♣ or 4♦). So, the responses are in single steps, showing 0, 1, 2, 3 or 4 key cards counting one step at a time including 4NT and 5m as active steps in the count as far as responder is concerned.

Responder does not have an option to overrule the enquiry and sign-off himself. Having assessed responder's key card count, the enquirer is the only party with a licence to abort the process by signing off at 4NT or 5m. Responder should not question this sign-off or carry on unilaterally.

The enquirer may follow with a trump-Queen enquiry and/or side-Kings enquiry, which we will discuss specifically shortly.

When replying to MSRKCB, responder does not attempt to show a void.

13.6 Step-responses to trump-Queen enquiry in Exclusion and MSRKCB

In both Exclusion-RKCB and MSRKCB, following the initial key card enquiry and the response, the next available forcing step is a trump-Queen enquiry. In MSRKCB this obviously excludes 4NT or 5m as active steps because those two bids are reserved as optional sign-off spots for the enquirer.

Because the original starting point was variable and the initial key card response was on a straight steps principle, I think it logically follows that in both Exclusion-RKCB and MSRKCB the responses to the trump-Queen enquiry should also be on a straight steps principle from where the first round of enquiry left us.

In addition, when he has the trump-Queen responder can also indicate his side-King count in one breath, as follows:

Step 1 reply	No trump-Queen
Step 2 reply	Trump-Queen but no side-King
Step 3 reply	Trump-Queen plus 1 side-King
Step 4 reply	Trump-Queen plus 2 side-Kings
Step 5 reply (in MSRKCB only)	Trump-Queen plus 3 side-Kings

13.7   Step-responses to side-Kings enquiry in Exclusion and MSRKCB

If following a negative response to a trump-Queen enquiry, the asking bid for side Kings will be the next available forcing step.

But at times the enquirer will not need to have enquired about the trump-Queen in the first place because either she has the Queen herself already or because she knows or suspects a 10-card fit and so anticipates the Queen to drop. So she may directly move on to ask about side Kings after the initial key card enquiry. In these cases she will skip to the second available forcing step to distinguish an immediate side Kings enquiry.

Again because the responses to the original key card enquiry (and to any follow-on Trump-Queen enquiry) will have been on a straight steps principle. I think it would again be consistent if in both Exclusion-RKCB and MSRKCB the responses to the side Kings enquiry were to be also be on a straight steps principle, as follows:

Step 1 reply	No side Kings
Step 2 reply	1 side-King
Step 3 reply	2 side-Kings
Step 4 reply (in MSRKCB only)	3 side-Kings

13.8   Our RKCB matrix

The starting points under the three different RKCB conventions I covered are different by nature.   Because the regular RKCB sequences always starts with 4NT, we are on auto pilot with the 5♣ and 5♦ responses and the composite key card counts which these represent, in our case 4/1 and 3/0, respectively.   But the starting point is variable with Exclusion RKCB and MSRKCB. To reiterate the fact that there are no stock answers this time, I find it safer in these cases to use key card count responses on a one-step-at-a-time basis, starting with zero for the first step.

Having made that distinction with the first round responses, it seems logical and consistent to me to continue with the trump-Queen and side-Kings responses in Exclusion RKCB and MSRKCB also on a one-step-at-a-time basis, starting with a negative reply for the first step. So I like to use the either/or replies for trump-Queen and side-Kings specifically and only for the main/regular RKCB sequences.

Here is a summary table for my suggested RKCB methods:

Version	Start	Reply	Q-ask	Reply	K-ask	Reply
Regular RKCB	4NT	composite	next	either/or	5NT	either/or
Exclusion-RKCB	5x	steps	next	steps	next	steps
Minor-suit RKCB	4m	steps	next	steps	next	steps

13.9 When opponents interfere with our RKCB

It is important to have clearly agreed methods to deal with opponents' intervention over our RKCB asking bids, whether they double or overcall. I find the following response structure most logical and equally applicable in all versions of RKCB we may be using:

Pass	1st step reply of our relevant response system
Double/Redouble	2nd step reply of our relevant response system
Next step over intervention	3rd step reply of our relevant response system
Second next step	4th step reply of our relevant responses, etc

Responder uses the same principles whether the asking bid was for key cards or the trump-Queen or side-Kings.

It is best to ignore opponents' doubles of our responses. The enquirer is more likely to want to get on with any further enquiry she had in mind, in which case she will choose the appropriate next forcing step for the relevant follow-on enquiry. But if she was minded to sign-off anyway. she should not be averse to an opportune pass of any double in case responder can turn the situation into an advantage by perhaps redoubling to show or confirm first round control there, failing which he can of course always do the signing-off from his side.

Chapter 14

Two-suited Hands

Two-suited hands can have great playing strength with relatively few high card points. It is imperative to make most of them in the bidding and investigate our full potential whether we open the bidding or we overcall.

14.1 Our 2-suited overcalls

After opponents open 1 of a suit, there are 3 two-suited combinations that an overcaller may want to show in the remaining suits. Allowing for 4 different suits in which the opponents may have opened, there can be 12 different two-suited combinations or 24 scenarios involving one or the other of the two overcall suits. Clearly it would be an advantage to be able to indicate precisely which two suits you have for your overcall in one shot.

All 2-suited overcall conventions have their drawbacks. The most common methods are:

- Michaels/UNT: Cue minor = majors; Cue major = other M + m; 2N = minors

- CRO (Colour-Rank-Other): Cue = same colour; 2N = same rank; 3♣ = others

- Ghestem: Cue-bid = highest and lowest suits; 2N = 2 lowest; 3♣ = 2 highest

- Questem: Cue-bid = 2 highest suits; 2N = 2 lowest; 3♣ = highest and lowest

Michaels and the related Unusual-2-No-Trumps overcalls have the following two problems (which the others don't have):

First, when we show a specific major and an unspecified minor, partner may have a problem if he has mediocre support for the major and just one reasonable minor. Should he play it safe and bid the major or take a chance at finding an excellent minor suit fit? This ambiguity about the minor suit affects 4 possible cases out of the 24 possible scenarios.

Second, we cannot show all hand types. Specifically, we cannot show a hand with spades and a minor at all if the other minor is opened. This problem affects another 2 overcalls (or 4 of our 24 total scenarios, keeping all our comparisons on the same basis).

On the other hand CRO, Ghestem and Questem all have the following problem (which Michaels/UNT doesn't have):

We lose 3♣ as a weak jump overcall or whatever it means in our system. This could be significant and it does affect 1/3rd of all cases under each of these three conventions.

CRO and Questem. but not Ghestem, have an additional smaller problem:

In situations where clubs is one of your two suits in a strong two-suited hand you cannot use the 3♣-overcall because partner may pass. Instead you would have to double first and possibly struggle to show your two-suited hand type in later bidding. This may not be a huge problem as the incidence of a strong two-suited overcall is fairly rare.

A final comparison can be made in terms of the ability to sign off at the 2-level. the practical lowest sign-off level after opponents open the bidding.

All four systems compare reasonably well in terms of the number of 2-level sign-offs available. but not all suits get an equal chance in each system. Notably. Ghestem avails the fewest 2-level contracts (equal fewest with CRO) and fewer still in the majors. The comparison under this criterion is as follows:

- Michaels/UNT: Six 2-level contracts possible out of 24; 4 in 2♠ and 2 in 2♥

- CRO: Four 2-level contracts possible; 2 in 2♠, 1 in 2♥, 1 in 2♦

- Ghestem: Four 2-level contracts possible; 3 in 2♠, 1 in 2♦

- Questem: Five 2-level contracts possible; 2 in 2♠ and 3 in 2♥

So which is the best 2-suited overcall convention overall?

If we are not prepared to sacrifice our normal 3♣ jump overcall then there is only Michaels/UNT available. But this comes with no bid in 2 situations and it is ambiguous in the minors in 4 situations. These significant limitations ought to rule out Michaels/UNT.

Assuming that we are prepared to use 3♣ conventionally then the choice is between the other three. I think that Ghestem loses out slightly because it enables one of the fewest 2-level final contracts and none in hearts.

This seems to narrow it down to CRO or Questem, both involving the small disadvantage (CRO in 4 cases and Questem in 3 cases) that 3♣ is not an option with strong two-suited hands which include the ♣-suit itself (and so a double is the only way to start those hands). If this does not put us off too much then we are nearly there!

Between these two, Questem is superior to CRO in enabling more 2-level sign-offs (5 v 4 cases) of which more are in the majors suits (5 v 3). So, well, Questem it is!

Direct cue-bid:	2 highest ranking suits
2NT:	2 lowest ranking suits
3♣:	highest and lowest ranking suits

Or more specifically, the complete range is as follows:

(1♣)-2♣	♠ and ♥ (two highest)
(1♣)-2N	♦ and ♥ (two lowest)
(1♣)-3♣	♠ and ♦ (highest and lowest)
(1♦)-2♦	♠ and ♥ (two highest)
(1♦)-2N	♣ and ♥ (two lowest)
(1♦)-3♣	♣ and ♠ (highest and lowest)
(1♥)-2♥	♠ and ♦ (two highest)
(1♥)-2N	♣ and ♦ (two lowest)
(1♥)-3♣	♠ and ♣ (highest and lowest)
(1♠)-2♠	♥ and ♦ (two highest)
(1♠)-2N	♣ and ♦ (two lowest)
(1♠)-3♣	♥ and ♣ (highest and lowest)

The overcall should show at least 5-5 shape (not 6-4 or 5-4, although Questem is less likely to get into trouble with 5-4 in majors than some other methods).

It is best to play the system as 'weak or strong' (6-10 HCP or 16+ HCP). Very weak hands with no prospect of buying the contract should avoid coming-in as this gives away very specific information to the opponents if they end up declaring the hand. The 3♣ jump overcall should be avoided with strong hands which include the ♣-suit as one of the two suits as this risks partner passing. All intermediate-strength hands make a normal overcall in the higher ranking suit and hope for a chance to bid the other suit later.

14.2 Leaping and Non-Leaping Michaels overcalls

Whilst Questem takes the prize for me for 2-suited overcalls over opponent's 1-level opening bids, I think Leaping-Michaels has no rival over opponent's weak 2-openings.

The basic idea here is that a jump overcall to 4♣ or 4♦ over an opponent's weak-2 major opener shows a strong 2-suited hand comprising the other major and the minor shown. Partner/advancer chooses between pass, 4-major or 5-minor. I would suggest that a 4NT reply should act as RKCB for the minor initially although the advancer may later settle in the major.

The leap to 4-minor also applies over opponents' weak 2♦-openers, this time 4♦ obviously showing both majors and 4♣ showing clubs along with a major. In the latter case the advancer can continue with 4♦ to ask which major the overcaller holds.

Over an opponent's multi-2♦ opener, always to be treated initially as a weak-2 in one of the majors, the system works similarly. 4♣ shows clubs and a major and 4♦ now shows diamonds and a major. In the former case advancer can continue with 4♦ to ask about the overcaller's major, whereas in the latter case 4♥ would act as 'pass or correct'. There is no point in waiting for the opponents to clarify their major because they may suddenly bid up to the 4-level in their suit before we get another look in.

Indeed, I don't see any reason why the 2-suited Leaping-Michaels 4-minor overcalls cannot be used over opponents' Muiderberg or Lucas style 2-level weak openers. Those being 2-suited openings themselves there is in fact more chance of the overcaller having the other 2 suits in a distributional hand. Opponents' anchor suit can be treated as their 'main' suit for the purpose of choosing our Leaping-Michael overcall suit. Easy!

In fact such is the effectiveness of Leaping-Michaels overcalls over opponents' 2-level weak openings that the same idea extends to 'non-leaping' Michaels overcalls over opponents' weak 3-level opening bids. A 4-level minor suit overcall would rarely be needed as a competitive bid - you would either bid 5 or make a take-out double to keep the majors in the frame. So, a 4-level non-leaping Michaels overcall to show 5-5 distribution and game-values is rational and has reasonable frequency, leaving a double to show tolerance for all 3 other suits.

So the full scheme of Leaping and Non-leaping Michaels 4-level overcalls over opponents' 2 and 3-level pre-empts look like this:

(2M)-4m	The minor shown plus the other major
(3m)-4m cue	Both majors
(3♣)-4♦ jump	♦+M (→ 4♥: pass-or-correct)
(3♦)-4♣ non-jump	♣+M (→ 4♦: which major?)
(3M)-4m non-jump	The minor shown plus the other major

The system also applies against opponents' other two-suited and/or weak pre-emptive openings:

Over Lucas and Muiderberg 2s: treat their anchor suit as weak pre-empt

Over Multi-2♦: 4♣= ♣+M (→ 4♦ which M?); 4♦ = ♦+M (→ 4♥ pass/correct)

Over weak-2♦: 4♣ = ♣+M (→ 4♦ which major?); 4♦ = both majors

14.3   When   opponents   make   a   2-suited overcall

Are you making the most of the additional bids which opponents' 2-suited overcalls make available to you? They provide an opportunity for fine-tuning our own bidding. Here's a very playable scheme:

If their 2-suited overcall specifies both of their suits, then our cue-bid of the cheaper of their suits is a good raise in partner's suit but a direct raise of partner's suit is weaker. That much is standard. The only point to make here is that the 'cheaper' suit is not necessarily the 'lower-ranking' suit; if an opponent overcalls our 1♥ bid with 2♥ showing specifically spades and diamonds then the spade suit is cheaper to cue-bid than the diamond suit.

I like the idea that our cue-bid of their other, more-expensive suit shows 5+ cards in the fourth suit and is forcing; so a direct simple bid of the fourth suit itself is a non-forcing competitive bid.

Double of their specific 2-suited overcall shows intent to penalise at least one of their suits, but partner should take it out if weak or distributional. Once doubled, all of our subsequent doubles of their run-out bids are also for penalties.

If on the other hand their 2-suited overcall shows one anchor suit and an unspecified second suit, then we have fewer specific bids available. Our cue bid of their anchor suit is a good raise of partner's suit whereas a direct raise of partner's suit is a weaker raise.

This time with their second suit unknown, it is best to actually name any new suit of interest to us. Our new suit bid here will be forcing, especially if we are introducing a major suit.

A double of their 2-suited overcall with only one of the suits known must be a general competitive double showing interest in the remaining two suits and some tolerance for partner's suit.

14.4 2-suited intervention to opponents' strong-♣ systems

This chapter seems to be the appropriate place also to mention my preferred defensive 2-suited overcalls when opponents open the bidding with a strong-1♣. I refer to Precision or similar artificial strong club systems here but not to such systems as Polish Club which often unravel as a weak-NT hand type with their first rebid.

The basic premise is that you need either shape or points to interfere when opponents open the bidding. In cases where they announce particular strength at the outset you are more likely to be coming into the bidding with shape if at all.

In principle I like Truscott type overcalls when opponents open with a strong-1♣. In this scheme simple overcalls show the suit you bid plus the next suit up the line (and clubs go with hearts and diamonds go with spades to complete the pairings and assign meanings to a double and 1NT overcall).

In practice I like to tweak the original Truscott system in two respects. Firstly, I think 5-4 or 4-5 shape for our two suits should be good enough, rather than the originally envisaged 5-5. The lesser requirement increases the frequency considerably. So the suit you bid could be 4 or 5-cards but also confirms 5 or 4-cards in the next suit up.

Secondly, I prefer to double their 1♣ opening with my club-heart combination but double their artificial 1♦ reply with my diamond-spade combination. Doubling their named suit (albeit an artificial suit) when holding that same suit in my hand comes more naturally. So, that leaves our 1NT overcall of their 1♣ to show a diamond-spade combination and our 1NT overcall of their artificial 1♦ reply to show a club-heart combination.

All our 2-suited simple overcalls are of indeterminate strength, but in practice usually weak. An unlikely stronger overcaller can bid again. All our jump overcalls are weak 6-card suits. Here's the full menu:

(1♣*)-x	Clubs and hearts
→ 1♦	Diamonds and hearts
→ 1♥	Hearts and spades
→ 1♠	Spades and clubs
→ 1N	Diamonds and spades
→ 2♣	Clubs and diamonds
→ 2♦/♥/♠	Weak, 6+ card suit

(1♣)-p-(1♦)-x	Diamonds and spades
→ → → 1♥	Hearts and spades
→ → → 1♠	Spades and clubs
→ → → 1N	Clubs and hearts
→ → → 2♣	Clubs and diamonds
→ → → 2♦	Diamonds and hearts
→ → → 2M	Weak, 6+ card suit

Chapter 15

Competitive Tools

Here I present a selection of gadgets for use in competitive auctions. Some you will have come across before although you may not have played them yourself. Others are less mainstream, and there are also some with my personal touch about them.

15.1 Composite negative and support doubles

This is a method of doubling which combines negative doubles and support doubles.

My idea with this composite structure is that negative doubles will apply in the usual way if there is still an unclaimed major, but

support doubles and redoubles will apply if both majors have already
been bid or implied by either side. If opponents double our major
we take it that their double represents an implied claim for the other
major even if their system does not necessarily always promise the
other major.

This composite idea starts with and builds on Eric Rodwell's support
doubles. The main support double/redouble positions, universally
played, are:

- Minor-(Pass/Double)-Major-(Other Major)-Double

- Minor-(Pass/Double)-Major-(Double)-Redouble

- Minor-(Pass/Double)-Major-(Other Minor at 2-level)-Double

- Major-(Pass/Double)-Other major-(Minor at 2-level)-Double

- Major-(Pass/Double)-Other major-(Double)-Redouble

In all the above sequences opener's rebid (double or redouble) shows
3-card support for responder's major, whereas a direct raise would
have shown exactly 4-card support. Incidentally the direct raise is
also alertable because it specifically shows 4-cards.

Support doubles/redoubles only apply when the next opponent
intervenes after partner responded in a major and his response
promised no longer than the regulation length in the suit, i.e. it
could be just a 4-card suit. Thus it is usually the case that the first
opponent would have passed our opening bid or doubled it rather
than overcall in a suit.

Over any suit overcall by the first opponent, all suit bids by our
responder would already be showing a 5-card suit, so in those cases
opener can raise with 3-card support rather than double. The only

exception comes after a 1♣-(1♦) start when responder's double specifically shows 4-4 in the majors and so any major-suit response instead in this case could still be on a 4-card suit and therefore here the support double/redouble mechanism remains applicable for opener's rebid.

Support doubles/redoubles apply only up to the 2-level in responder's major. Support doubles/redoubles are opener's rebids only - they do not apply to responder and they do not apply in any position other than opener's first rebid position.

When a choice of rebids are available (maybe a stopper-showing NT-rebid, or a reverse bid, or a rebid of opener's own suit, along with the option of showing 3-card support for responder), it often works well if opener prioritises the support double/redouble - there may yet be time later to pass on the message about the other features.

The fact of a 3-card fit enables responder to compete up to the level of fit in the subsequent bidding. Sometimes we end up in a 4-3 fit at the 2-level (if next opponent passes and responder does not have 1NT available) but that rarely spells disaster.

Playing pure support doubles, after a start such as 1♦-(p)-1♥-(2♣), a double by opener would show 3-card support for responder's major but a fit in the unclaimed major may escape notice. There could be other similar examples depending on whether we agree to bring a diamond response into the system or how opponents play their doubles of our major.

My composite alternative fixes this kind of problem. So I suggest that a double/redouble by opener as her rebid should retain the usual 'negative' meaning as an override so long as there remains a major not yet claimed by an actual bid or an implied double by either side. So, after 1♦-(p)-1♥-(2♣), a double shows spades first and foremost. Similarly, after 1♦-(p)-1♠-(2♣), a double shows hearts as the primary message rather than 3-card spade support.

The composite negative-and-support-double retains all the fundamentals of the support double/redouble mechanism but also avoids missing a better fit in the other major.

If you have not tried support doubles before because you did not want to give up on your usual negative doubles, then this composite structure means you can play both.

15.2   When opponents double our Stayman, FSF or NMF bids

When an opponent doubles an asking bid of ours, usually for lead-directing purposes, this does not have to be a disadvantage.

At high-level cue bidding, the usual counter-measure is to redouble to show first-round control or pass to deny it. A pass allows partner a turn to redouble it with a first-round control there.

What about their lower-level doubles? I have in mind our everyday asking bids such as:

• Stayman enquiry, our 2♣ over 1NT, or 3♣ over 2NT

• Any Fourth Suit Forcing enquiry at 2 or 3-level

- Checkback or New Minor Forcing 2♣/♦ over 1NT, or 3♣/♦ over 2NT

We can turn their double even in these cases into an advantage for ourselves if we establish some general parameters (in addition to any specific counters against specific doubles).

The first thing to say is that their double of our artificial bid gives our responder extra bids, namely pass and redouble, as well as our normal system responses to the enquiry.

Pass is an interesting one. After the opponents double our enquirer will now get another bid whether or not our responder passes the double. But it would be a waste of a call if responder just uses his pass to mean "I have nothing to say". He has a free bid and whatever he calls the bidding will continue. What's more, after passing the first time, he will still get another bite at the cherry when our enquirer bids to keep the bidding still open.

So, pass may as well mean something useful on the part of our responder and it works best if, as a counter to the double, pass in fact shows a stopper in the attacked artificial suit. As a corollary, if responder bids on ignoring the double this now denies a stop. So, we have:

- Pass: Stopper(s) in the artificial suit

- Bid on: No stopper and bidding on as if opponent did not double

If responder is passing then how do we get back on track, you might ask. Assuming that the next opponent is also passing, all our enquirer needs to do is simply redouble, which now enables responder to resume the sequence!

So. having additionally clarified his position in the attacked suit, responder now gets to respond to the original enquiry as well after all.

Responder should pass originally to show the attacked suit position in preference even when he has a positive response to the original enquiry. such as a major suit to disclose in response to Stayman. This is because he will still get a turn to give the system response the next time.

This detour to indicate the presence or absence of a stopper in the attacked suit may later enable the hand to be played in no-trumps or in any event allow us to better judge our prospects in marginal game-going situations even in suit-contracts.

If responder bids on after opponent's double, the implicit denial of any stopper in the attacked suit is also very useful information. So, for example. the enquirer will now be unlikely to choose no-trumps as a final contract. or do so only in the full knowledge that responder will not be contributing to stopping that suit.

Here's a more specific list of responder's options including some redoubles after an opponent doubles our specific asking bids:

When an opponent doubles partner's 2♣ Puppet Stayman (and similarly for 3♣ Puppet Stayman):

- Pass shows club stop(s) (→ redouble from partner reconvenes Puppet)

- 2♦ denies a club stop and confirms at least one 4-card major

- 2M denies a club stop and shows a 5 card major

When an opponent doubles partner's Fourth Suit Forcing bid:

- Pass shows stop(s) in fourth suit ($\rightarrow$ partner redoubles to reconvene)

- Rebidding a suit shows extra shape and denies a stop in fourth suit

- Redouble denies a stop in fourth suit and also denies extra shape

When an opponent doubles partner's 2♣, 2♦, 3♣, 3♦ New Minor Forcing bid:

- Pass shows stop(s) in that minor ($\rightarrow$ partner redoubles to resume bidding)

- Ignoring the double to reply NMF enquiry denies a stop in the minor

- Redouble denies a stop in the minor or anything to add in the majors

Taking the opportunity of the opponents' suit-showing doubles at low-levels and turning it on its head to clarify our winners/stoppers in the threatened suit in this way seems to me to be more useful, or at least of more frequent use, than other methods of dealing with attacks on our low-level artificial asking bids, especially with the added pleasure in our system of being able to resume our intended sequence thereafter without loss.

This scheme is intended as a 2 or 3-level manoeuvre to help judge the best ultimate contract. It should not apply to opponents' lead-directing doubles of our higher level cue-bids, fourth suit forcing bids, RKCB or MSRKCB sequences. Nor should it apply to opponents' doubles of our transfers because there a pass is more useful to show less than 3 cards support.

15.3   Switched meanings of pass and double when they cue-bid our suit

Another simple but very effective competitive tool is to switch our meanings of pass and double when opponents cue-bid our suit. That is, double when one might have passed; but pass when one would have normally doubled.

I am thinking more about the low-level cue-bid situations by opponents, usually to show a good raise of their own suit or to ask for a stopper in ours.

In normal bidding when you double their cue-bid to reassure partner or give the usual agreed positive message, the next opponent gets two extra chances - he can now redouble or pass. At low-level bidding their redouble might show extras if not a control in the suit and their pass might mean that this opponent has nothing to add. At higher-levels the first opponent is more likely to redouble to show first-round control or pass to deny it and give the other opponent a chance. Either way the opponents are given new lines of communication between them.

But if you switch the meanings as I suggest then your pass will give your good news to partner and the next opponent cannot double a pass! Instead he now has to commit their side because he does not have the option of passing his own partner's cue-bid in our suit either.

The positive message for your pass could be whatever your double in your previous agreements would have meant. Maybe this could be reassuring partner that you have a top-3 honour card and so she can lead the suit (if she had bid it) or that you are quite happy with your own suit quality (if you had bid it).

Conversely, your switched-meaning double could now be giving partner a negative message to deny any help with her suit (if it was partner's suit) or that are not very proud of your own holding (if it was your own suit). It is a cost-nothing double even if only to lower partner's expectations from you in the suit.

Moreover, your negative-message double will not necessarily provide the next opponent with any clear new options in what is probably an un-discussed reverse-bidding situation for them.

It is important to be mutually clear that this reversing of the usual message between our doubles and passes applies only to the first person to bid from our side immediately after their cue-bid of our suit.

We do not both have to have bid the suit - it is sufficient that only one of us has bid the suit in which the opponents now cue-bid. Just like when in normal bidding one of us shows a suit and whether the other raises it or not an opponent may cue-bid the suit usually to show a good raise in their earlier suit or to ask for a stopper in our suit. So it is just like before - except that now we show reverse-attitude to their cue-bid!

Playing 1♣ opening as a 2+ card suit, we can also apply this switch mechanism to opponents' cue-bid in the club suit, but not to their natural rebid attempts in the suit. When it is clearly not their suit and they are cue-bidding in it, we can use the system to clarify our own position with the suit.

There is no reason why the new system should not apply also to opponents' other artificial bids in our suit at high-levels, even in their RKCB sequences.

15.4 Transfer advances following partner's overcall

When the opponents open the bidding and partner overcalls, usually you as advancer have ways of differentiating between a good raise and a weak raise of partner's suit and a new suit is normally played as constructive (maybe with tolerance for partner's suit).

Transfer-advances simply involve a re-arrangement of the bids available to the advancer. Keeping no-trumps bids as natural, suit bids become transfers generally in a circle (with clubs sitting above spades). As part of this scheme, a transfer to partner's suit (rather than a cue bid) now shows a strong-raise whilst a direct raise remains a weaker raise.

Here is how it works:

(1♣)-1♠-(p)-1N				Natural (lowest-NT bid by advancer remains natural)
→	→	→	2♣*	Shows diamonds, indeterminate values
→	→	→	2♦*	Shows hearts, indeterminate values
→	→	→	2♥*	Good transfer raise to 2♠ with 3-card support
→	→	→	2♠	Weaker or distributional raise with 3-card support

We have retained two alternative ways of raising partner's overcall. But the difference is that now we have also introduced a way for the advancer to bring in a biddable suit of his own without committing himself whether he means this to be forcing or non-forcing. He can play it both ways because the completion of the transfer gives him another bid.

The overcaller, unless holding a very big hand, will simply complete the transfer - which does not imply a fit - and the advancer can pass this out if he is weak with a long suit. So the system enables an advancer with no tolerance for overcaller's suit but a reasonable long suit of his own and some 6-7 HCP to come in and buy the contract, which is usually impossible.

At other times with a strong hand instead, the advancer just continues bidding over partner's completion of the transfer with a new descriptive bid - maybe a return to overcaller's suit to show Hx in an invitational hand or cue-bid opponent's suit as a stopper-asking bid, and so on.

My above example sequence was clear-cut because partner's overcall was in the most 'expensive' suit and bypassed the other 2 suits. The transfer-advances work best when the advancer wants to introduce a suit that was bypassed by the overcaller.

It is possible to keep to the same methods every time but there is really no advantage in playing transfers to suits which the overcaller did NOT bypass. In fact a hybrid system seems best which retains natural advancer bids for non-bypassed suits. For instance:

(1♥)-2♣-(p)-2♦		Natural (because overcaller did not bypass diamonds)
→	→ → 2♥*	Shows spades, indeterminate values
→	→ → 2♠*	Good transfer raise to 3♣ with 4-card fit (bid to level of fit)
→	→ → 2N	Natural (lowest-level NT-bid by advancer remains natural)
→	→ → 3♣	Weaker or distributional raise with 4-card support

In the matrix of possible 1-level suit openings by an opponent and possible non-jump overcalls by partner, 12 cases in all, there will be 4 cases where the other 2 suits are both bypassed, 4 cases where neither are bypassed, and 4 cases where 1 is bypassed and the other not. That is to say, half the time the transfer advance system will apply and half the time it will not.

It is not particularly difficult to work out when the system applies. As soon as partner makes an overcall, you just need to recall which suits if any have been bypassed and so will need the transfer treatment.

It is never more costly to show a new suit with transfer advances compared to natural methods - it involves bidding the actual suit (when partner's overcall did not bypass it) or the suit below it (if partner bypassed it). The transfer cycle starts with opener's suit and finishes below the overcall suit.

When no suit is bypassed by the overcall, the transfer advance structure is one and the same as our more familiar natural bids and the use of the cue bid of their suit as a good-raise in ours.

The transfer advances are intended for no higher then the 3-level. Beyond that it may get complicated and conflict with some other useful conventions.

The system does not get disturbed and so remains on if the second opponent comes in with 1NT or a negative double. But the system is off if the second opponent raises the first opponent's suit or introduces a new suit (and in these cases the advancer reverts back to normal cue bids as a good raise).

There is one technical disadvantage in that if the overcaller becomes the declarer in the advancer's suit then the second opponent usually has an easy lead in the first opponent's suit.

Transfer advances do not create any new bidding space but rather rearrange it. The advantage is that the advancer can now introduce a new suit in competitive auctions and retain the option of a second bid, if not a pass, over the completion of the transfer.

15.5 3♣ intermediate opening bid

Do you find that a 3-level pre-empt in a minor, especially in clubs, does not seem to inconvenience the opponents all that much after all? I do. So, there is something to be said for some other use for a 3-level opening bid and I like 3♣ to show an intermediate hand, 11-14 HCP, with at least 6-clubs and denying a major.

There are many light-weight 3NT contracts to be bid when the club suit is running for 6 tricks between the two hands and I suggest the following scheme to investigate it:

3♣		Intermediate opening bid, 11-14 HCP, 6+ card suit
→ 3♦		Enquiry, Hxx or better ♣, invites 3N with 2 of 3 top honours
→ → 3♥	1 of top 3 honours, lower range, 11-12 HCP.
→ → 3♠	1 of top 3 honours, higher range, 13-14 HCP.
→ → 3N	2 of top 3 honours, irrespective of HCP-count
→ 3M	5+card suit, forcing

I think that responder's 3♥ or 3♠ is best played as forcing. With
anything less he may just as well pass 3♣.

An intermediate 3♣ opening bid also takes some pressure off the
short-1♣ opening bid, promising no more than a doubleton in the
suit. The corollary is that when opener starts with 1♣ and over
most 1-level replies jumps to 3♣ then this usually marks her with
17+ HCP and 6+ cards in the suit. After all with 15-16 HCP and a
6-card club suit, and 3-2-2 in the other three suits, she might have
opened 1NT in the first place.

Chapter 16

Fine-tuning

The methods I covered in the last chapter were a little off the beaten track and even included some of my own concoctions and so you would not have seen them all before. By contrast the methods I cover in this chapter are more mainstream and you may well be very familiar with most. They are included here for completeness of our system as I think these are indispensible fine-tuning tools.

16.1   Lebensohl

Lebensohl is a very useful convention to deal with opponents' weak-2 and similar opening bids which take away some of our bidding space before we start. In these situations we may have to double with less than the perfect shape for a takeout double.

When we double opponents' weak-2 opening bid for take-out, Lebensohl enables the advancer to distinguish between various hand types and strengths. The doubler can then judge the level of borderline hands better as well as the final denomination.

After partner's double, the advancer's 2-level suit bids above the rank of opener's suit, if available, are minimal bids promising no more than 4-cards and are not forward-going, with up to 7 HCP.

With a suit to show below the rank of opener's suit, following partner's double the advancer can sign-off at the 3-level by using 2NT as an artificial bid. Doubler relays the 2NT reply to 3♣ for advancer to pass this or to correct it to another suit below the rank of opponent's. That is the advancer's way of signing-off at the 3-level in suits that were not available at the 2-level.

Therefore there is no natural 2NT reply available to the advancer when partner doubles. This is the price for Lebensohl, but on grounds of frequency it is a price worth paying.

The fact of the relay sign-off via 2NT means that direct bids instead by the advancer at the 3-level below the opponent's suit now show 4+card suits in invitational hands, about 8-11 HCP.

If the advancer's suit was available at 2-level (for weak sign-off) and he first bypasses it to relay via 2NT but then bids that suit at 3-level, this logically now becomes an invitational bid in that suit. So, advancer's invitational bids go through the 2NT route when his suit is a higher ranking suit than the opponents' suit.

Direct 3-level jump bids in suits above the rank of opponents' suit are inevitably forcing bids offering the doubler a choice of games.

She may be able to raise the advancer's suit or bid 3NT with a stop in the opponent's suit. A very strong single-suited doubler would instead bid her own suit at this stage, even at the 4-level.

If the opponents had opened with a weak-2 in a major then, following partner's double, the advancer's cue-bid in that major would be Staymanic, showing the other major. In the sequence (2♦)-x-(p)-3♦ the advancer shows both majors.

The advancer has more room for precision when his suit is a higher ranking suit than the opponents' weak-2 suit. He can now distinguish not only between intermediate and forcing hands but even between 4-card and 5-card suits, depending on whether or not he cue-bids opponents' suit along the way. This's what I play when opponents open a weak-2♥ and partner doubles for take-out (which, let's say, can be done on 3 cards in the other major):

2♠	Weak, 0-7 HCP, 4+ spades
2N- 3♣-3♥	Intermediate, 8-11 HCP, 4 card spade suit
2N- 3♣-3♠	Intermediate, 8-11 HCP, 5 card spade suit
3♥	Forcing, 12+ HCP, 4 card spade suit
3♠	Forcing, 12+ HCP, 5 card spade suit

A strong advancer angling for 3NT rather than introduce his own suit also has two alternative routes to get to 3NT, which he can use to distinguish whether he has a stopper in the opponent's suit or not. I prefer a direct 3NT bid to show a stopper and a relay via 2NT to deny a stopper. So, in the sequence (2♥)-x-(p)-2NT-(p)-3♣-(p)-3NT the advancer says he is relying on the doubler for a heart-stop, failing which she should try her 4-card suits upwards.

The direct approach for the positive message is called FASS (Fast Arrival Shows Stopper). I like playing my Lebensohl the FASS way. It is also possible to play it the other way, FADS (Fast Arrival Denies Stopper). But FASS, the positive message being conveyed with direct and aggressive-sounding bids, comes more naturally to me.

To recap, after any weak-2 opener by opponents and a take-out double by partner, advancer's full menu is as follows:

- 2-level suit bid: 4+ suit, to play, 0-7 HCP

- 2NT: Relay to 3♣, pass-or-correct below their suit, to play, 0-7 HCP

- 3-level direct suit bids below their suit: 4+ suit, invitational, 8-11 HCP

- 3-level cue bid: Staymanic, 4 cards in other/both major(s)

- 3-level suit bid above their suit: 5+suit, forcing if direct, invitational via 2NT

- 3NT: Denies 4-card/other major, direct 3N shows stop, via 2N denies it

Lebensohl is primarily the advancer's way of distinguishing his hand types and values following partner's perhaps awkward double of the opponents' weak-2 openers. The advancer should cut some slack for partner's doubles in these situations and assume that it has perhaps 2 places to play, rather than all other 3 suits. Indeed she may be single-suited but perhaps just too strong to overcall simply. By inference, a simple overcall rather than a double marks the overcaller with a modest opening hand with a 5+card suit.

Lebensohl has many other applications. In addition to the primary situation in the sequence (2M)-x-(p)-2NT where opponent's 2M was a weak-major, I also like to play along the Lebensohl principles in all the following belated weak-2 situations:

- 1♥-(2♠)-p-(p)-x-(p)-2NT where opponent's 2♠ was a weak jump

- (1M)-p-(2M)-x-(p)-2NT where partner doubles their raise to 2M

- (1M)-x-(2M)-p-(p)-x-(p)-2NT where partner repeat-doubles their 2M sign-off

- (1M)-p-(2M)-p-(p)-x-(p)-2NT where partner protects over their 1-2M sign-off

- Generally when opponents open or bid to 2M and partner doubles for takeout

Lebensohl is also effective against opponents' multi-2♦ systems once it unravels as a weak-2 in a major. A double thereafter is no different than a double of an opening weak-2M bid in the first place and in response we can use the Lebensohl methods here just the same.

Lebensohl is equally valid facing opponents' essentially weak 2-suited opening bids anchored to one or the other major, such as Muiderberg and Lucas 2M openers. There is no reason why double/Lebensohl principles shouldn't apply here too, treating the opponents' bid as primarily a weak-2 in their anchor major suit.

It is in fact also common to play Lebensohl-type replies when an opponent intervenes with our side's 1NT opening bid. But in that specific situation I prefer Rubensohl instead, which was discussed on page 112 in Interference with our 1NT.

16.2   New Minor Forcing ('NMF')

When opener rebids 1NT after a response in a major it can be more effective for responder to use the unbid minor (rather than always 2♣) as checkback to clarify the mutual position in the majors. This will be 2♦ if partner had originally opened 1♣, but 2♣ if partner originally opened 1♦ or 1♥.

NMF has the merit of freeing up the 2♣ rebid by responder to become a natural non-forcing retreat when partner's opening bid was 1♣ and responder first had to show a major from a weak major-club combination. Similarly, responder can first show a major and then make a non-forcing 2♦ retreat when opener's opening bid was 1♦. Of course we open 1♦ when 4-4 in the minors but 1♣ when 3-3 or 2-3, without a 5-major major.

When the NMF asking bid is 2♣ (if partner originally opened 1♦ or 1♥) opener has 2♦ available as a negative reply (and 2NT here would be a positive reply).

When the NMF asking bid is 2♦ (if partner originally opened 1♣) then obviously opener no longer has the 2♦ step available in the response structure. In this case a 2NT reply by opener shows a weak hand with no features in the majors. But opener will still reply at 3-level with maximum HCP for her 1NT rebid with or without a feature in majors.

A feature in the majors means either at least one extra card than previously promised in one's own major, or 3-card support for responder's major (which had only promised 4-cards), or 4-cards in a major that has not yet been bid by either opener or responder.

By starting a NMF sequence responder promises invitational values of at least 11 HCP, enough to withstand opener to jump in reply to the 3-level with a maximum 14 HCP. If opener comes back with a minimum 2-level bid showing 12-13 HCP and no 3-card support for partner then a 2NT by responder is a sign-off. When opener shows a feature in her own major or in responder's major even at the 2-level (12-13 HCP) then responder's raise to 3M sets that major and shows slam interest. With anything less the responder would bid a fast-arrival 4M.

The start of a NMF checkback sequence by responder also implies that he has a feature in a major or in both majors or will make a strong return to opener's minor. Without any such features he would be passing or making an invitational raise in no-trumps or in opener's major, or even directly bidding game.

With features to show both in her own major and in responder's major, opener shows the feature in the lower-ranking major, hearts. If responder does not like the sound of that nor make a forcing return to opener's minor but just signs off in 2NT or 3NT, then opener can infer that responder's reason for the checkback was the other major, spades. So, if opener did have the requisite fit in spades after all he can now show it belatedly.

If over opener's 2♥ NMF-reply responder still wants to know if any fit is forthcoming for his spade suit then he needs jumps to 3♠ with a game-going hand, whereas I like to play a simple 2♠ as showing a minimum-NMF hand. In the latter case opener should pass with 3 card spade fit but convert it to 2NT with less.

If 1♦-1♠-1NT-2♣ is NMF and 1♦-1♠-1NT-2♦ is natural to play then logically it also follows that 1♦-1♠-1NT-3♣ is also natural to play. The last sequence shows that responder checked a spade fit first before having to fall back on his length in the 'other minor', presumably 4-6 shape in a weak hand, and does not seek correction back to spades. Similarly 1♣*-1♥*-1NT-3♦ is natural to play, allowing for transfer responses in the sequence.

New Minor Forcing principles work just the same at a level higher. 3♣ and 3♦ are NMF asking bids and now game-forcing when the opener rebids 2NT whether as a non-jump rebid (2-way, 12-14 or 18-19 HCP) or as a jump rebid (18-19 HCP).

If opponents double our NMF asking bid of 2♣, 2♦, 3♣, or 3♦, then:

- Pass shows stop(s) in that minor (→ partner redoubles to resume bidding)

- Ignoring the double to reply NMF enquiry denies a stop in the minor

- Redouble denies a stop in the minor or anything to add in the majors

New Minor Forcing is more versatile than 2♣ Staymanic or Crowhurst checkback methods. Here are some full NMF sequences following opener's 1NT rebid (12-14 HCP):

1♣-1♦*-1N-2♣	Natural to play (♣ was 2+ cards, ♦-reply showed ♥)
1♣-1♦*-1N-2♦	New Minor Forcing (♣ was 2+ cards, ♦-reply showed ♥)
→ → → → 2♥	Minimum, 3-card heart-fit, may still have 4 spades
→ → → → → 2♠	Responder 4-4 in majors, minimum for NMF (11 HCP)
→ → → → 2♠	Opener minimum, 4 spades, not 3 hearts, 4234 or 4225
→ → → → 2N	Minimum 12-13 HCP, no feature in majors, 3235 or 2245
→ → → → 3♣/♦	Maximum 14 HCP, no feature in majors, ♣:3235, ♦:2245
→ → → → 3♥/♠	Maximum 14 with major feature (3♥ may still have ♠)

1♣-1♥*-1N-2♣	Natural to play (♣ was 2+ cards, ♥-reply showed ♠)
1♣-1♥*-1N-2♦	New Minor Forcing (♣ was 2+ cards, ♥-reply showed ♠)
→ → → → 2♥	Minimum 12-13 HCP, 4 hearts, may still have 3 spades
→ → → → → 2♠	Responder has 5 spades, not 4 hearts, minimum NMF
→ → → → 2♠	Opener minimum 12-13, 3-card spade-fit, not 4 hearts
→ → → → 2N	Minimum 12-13 HCP, no feature in majors, 2335 or 2245
→ → → → 3♣/♦	Maximum 14 HCP, no feature in majors, ♣:2335, ♦:2245
→ → → → 3♥/♠	Maximum 14 with major feature (3♥ may still have ♠)

1♦- 1♥- 1N-2♦	Natural to play, responder unbalanced, heart-diamond
1♦- 1♥- 1N-2♣	New Minor Forcing (11+ HCP)
→ → → → 2♥	Minimum, 3-card heart-fit, may still have 4 spades
→ → → → → 2♠	Responder is 4-4 in majors, minimum for NMF (11 HCP)
→ → → → 2♠	Opener minimum, 4 spades, not 3 hearts, 4243 or 4252
→ → → → 2♦	Minimum 12-13, no feature in majors, 3244/3253/2254
→ → → → 2N	Maximum 14 HCP, no feature in majors, 3244 shape
→ → → → 3♣/♦	Maximum 14 HCP, no feature in majors, ♣:2254, ♦:3253
→ → → → 3♥/♠	Maximum 14 with major feature (3♥ may still have ♠)

1♦- 1♠- 1N-2♦	Natural to play, responder unbalanced, spade-diamond
1♦- 1♠- 1N-2♣	New Minor Forcing (11+ HCP)
→ → → → 2♥	Minimum 12-13 HCP, 4 hearts, may still have 3 spades
→ → → → → 2♠	Responder has 5 spades, not 4 hearts, minimum NMF
→ → → → 2♠	Opener minimum 12-13, 3-card spade-fit, not 4 hearts
→ → → → 2♦	Minimum 12-13, no feature in majors, 2353/2344/2254
→ → → → 2N	Maximum 14 HCP, no feature in majors, 2344 shape
→ → → → 3♣/♦	Maximum 14 HCP, no feature in majors, ♣:2254, ♦:2353
→ → → → 3♥/♠	Maximum 14 with major feature (3♥ may still have ♠)

1♦- 1♠- 1N- 3♣	To play, weak 4-6 in spades-clubs
1♣- 1♦*-1N- 3♦	To play, weak 4-6 in hearts-diamonds

16.3   Cue-bidding and 'serious 3NT'

These guidelines for cue-bidding, including the 'serious 3NT' treatment, and some notes on ace-asking principles are in the context of a 2-over-1 game-force environment.

In auctions where no fit has been confirmed, a 3-level bid of a new suit is not a control-showing cue-bid. Instead, it should be interpreted as a search for the right game. In the auction 1♥-2♦-2♥-3♣-3♠ you haven't agreed on a trump suit, so 3♠ cannot be a cue-bid. If you held spade values, you would have bid 3NT here, so the 3♠ bid is asking partner for a spade stop for no-trumps, failing which he should reply with the next best descriptive bid (and a 4m reply here would not be MSRKCB either).

Responder's 'low raise' (1♥-2♣-2NT-3♥) shows at least moderate extra values (14+ HCP and 3-card support) but it does not demand a cue-bid. Opener should make a cue-bid in this situation only if he has more than a dead minimum.

If after responder's agreement to opener's suit, opener then makes an early cue-bid in responder's 2-over-1 suit (1♥-2♣-2NT-3♥-4♣), it should show a fitting card (ace, king or queen), usually with moderate support (doubleton or better). It does not necessarily promise a first-round control. In the example sequence here opener should choose to show the fitting club honour (which could be the Queen) ahead of the diamond ace (but should not bypass the cheaper spade ace if she has it).

Other cue-bids show a first-round control (ace or void), bidding your cheapest control first. Bypassing a suit denies a control in that suit. In the auction 1♥-2♣-2NT-3♥-4♦ your 4♦ cue-bid shows the diamond ace and denies the spade ace or a club fitting-card.

I prefer to bid first round controls ahead of second round controls (not the Italian method of treating them as equal although I would agree that method has certain advantages too). So. for me. cue-bidding a new suit on a later occasion having bypassed it the first time round shows a second-round control (king or singleton).

If partner has bypassed a suit but is still showing some slam interest. you should cooperate where possible. In 1♥-2♣-2♥-3♥-4♣. opener has shown some life with 4♣. Responder knows opener does not have first round control in spades, but he can still cooperate even if he has no spade control either because opener might have second round control. So a 4♦ cue-bid by responder here does not imply that he has spades covered too but it does not deny it either (whereas 4NT by responder would imply at least second round stop in both spades and diamonds).

Over responder's 4♦ cue-bid, opener should probably sign off in 4♥ even if she has second-round spade control. In these situations the decision to go beyond 4♥ will typically be responder's. With a small doubleton in spades, or Qx. responder might decide that eleven tricks are safe and continue cue-bidding 5♣ or 5♦; but when responder also bypasses spades as he goes beyond 4♥ the position will now be clear to opener that she can only continue beyond 5♥ if she is looking at a second round spade control in her own hand.

After we find a major suit fit (1♥-2♣-2♥-3♥) or reach agreement by responder's simple preference or possibly false preference (1♠-2♥-3♣-3♠). since we would no longer choose to play in 3NT as a final contract, a bid of 3NT now shows serious intent for slam ('serious

3NT') and demands a cue-bid from partner.

The corollary to this 'serious 3NT' treatment is that, after any major-suit agreement by partner (and unless you are dead minimum in which case the fast-arrival principle applies), even when you do not have any slam ambitions yourself you should now always cue bid a first round control if you have one on the way to bidding game in the major with all remaining normal hands types (13+ HCP). This is called a 'courtesy cue-bid' which shows no extra values at all but is showing courtesy to partner in case he has.

So, after 1♠-2♣-2♠-3♠, the next bid indicates suitability for slam:

3NT	'Serious 3NT', slam-going hand in spades, demanding a cue-bid
3♣/4♦/4♥	Courtesy cue-bids promising no extras (not serious about slam)
4♠	Absolutely minimum

The position may look less clear after 1♥-2♣-2♥-3♥ because 3♠ is now also available below 3NT. Playing 3NT as 'serious' it is more consistent to treat everything else as non-serious, so 3♠ as well as 4♣ and 4♦ are courtesy cue-bids when the agreed major is hearts.

'Serious 3NT' and its corollary courtesy cue-bids can be started by either side, its entire pre-requisite being that it follows immediately after 3-level major suit agreement.

The idea with the strong hand demanding a cue-bid, rather than making one, is that partner will usually have less to show and so one single cue-bid (or lack of it) from that hand may resolve the situation early, whilst the stronger hand remains undisclosed.

4NT following some cue-bidding is still RKCB. If partner starts a cue-bidding sequence and later chooses to bypass 4NT in favour of more cue-bidding, this is often because specific first and/or second round controls are more relevant than the mere number of controls and so you should cooperate with partner's preference for more cue-bidding.

4NT by responder is not RKCB if it is bid directly over opener's first rebid of 2NT or 3NT. For example 1♠-2♣-2NT-4NT is quantitative, soliciting 6NT if opener has a maximum hand.

4NT by opener is not RKCB if she rebids 2NT and then raises 3NT to 4NT. As we discussed on page 26 in 2/1 Game-force, 1♠-2♣-2NT-3NT-4NT is the 2/1 system's way of showing a balanced 18-19 HCP hand because 2NT was initially a two-way bid (12-14 HCP or 18-19 HCP).

A double-jump in a new suit after explicit or implicit suit agreement is specifically Exclusion-RKCB when a single-jump would have been a regular splinter. For example, 1♥-2♦-2♥-4♠ (or 5♣) is RKCB excluding the double-jump suit, with hearts agreed as trumps.

A raise or return to 4 of a minor is never an invitational bid. Either it is an escape to a contract which stands some chance (maybe having investigated 3NT to no avail); or it is a constructive, clearly forward-going bid, in which case it is MSRKCB.

As it is almost cost-free, MSRKCB ought to be routinely tried in hands with a minor-suit flavour and some extras, signing off in 4NT or 5m if the first round MSRKCB-reply is not good enough.

16.4   5NT Grand Slam Force or Pick-A-Slam

With a known fit, a jump bid to 5 no-trumps in a sequence such as
1♥-3♥-5NT is an enquiry about partner's top three honours in the
trump suit. It implies that the other suits are under control. GSF
is usually played with a fit in a major suit only.

If there has been no express suit agreement and/or when both
partners have shown a suit, 5NT GSF implies agreement on the
last bid suit (so partner's suit) as in 1♥-2♦-3♥-5NT or in 4♠-5NT.

The basic response structure in Ely Culbertson's 1936 creation, then
called Josephine, was as follows:

6-level below trumps	None of the top 3 honours
6-trumps	1 of the top 3 honours
7-trumps	2 of the top 3 honours

Clearly the GSF-bidder needs to have a top-3 honour of her own to
commit to the 6-level in the first place.

It is possible to allocate more specific meanings to the 6-level bids
below the trump suit in order to differentiate between 3-card
support, longer-fit, trump-Queen and higher honour-card.   More
space is available when the trump suit is spades whereas with
hearts it would be necessary to merge some responses. But I am
not convinced that any more complication is justified to the
original structure which is easy to remember as it stands and seems
perfectly adequate for the infrequent use of GSF.

Let's not forget also the more common modern day use of the 5NT bid as a 'pick-a-slam' bid. There should be no mix-up because the circumstances for the latter use of the 5NT bid should be clear, which are primarily as follows:

Without a known fit, or in a case of 3 suits bid by the partnership, or when the opponents interfere with the auction, a jump to 5NT can be used to ask partner to pick the best slam. For example, after 1♦-1♥-2♠-3♥-3NT, responder with enough values and maybe a 3-6-2-1 shape could bid 5NT to offer a slam in any of the 3 suits. Or, after (2♥)-2♠-(4♥)-5♦-(p)-p-(5♥), advancer's 5NT probably shows a strong 2-1-6-4 hand and looking for the right slam.

When there is clearly no suit set and there exists some element of doubt about the final denomination, yet the hand is strong and adaptable to play in more than one place including some suits not even yet mentioned, 5NT neatly says 'pick-a-slam'.

Chapter 17

Opening Lead

The choice of what card to lead as you kick off the defence is obviously critical. Sometimes the relative fortunes of the defence and the declarer will irrecoverably depend on the opening lead. At other times it will give the tempo to one side or the other if not immediately determine the entire outcome. You will also want to re-assess the declaring side's bidding to decide whether to make a passive lead or an attacking lead. On occasions you will have very little defence in your own hand and so maybe try to set up partner's cards instead. Those decisions are yours to make.

What I will try to do in this section is perhaps add a little to your armoury to make the most of your lead whatever lead strategy you decide.

17.1 Ace for attitude, King for count

It seems to me that the 'standard' opening lead methods associated with SAYC and 2/1 systems do not necessarily make the most of the situations where you are fortunate enough to have both the Ace and the King in a suit. It seems that the only deviation allowed from leading the top card in any honours sequence is when you hold specifically doubleton touching-honours on lead against a suit contract. I find this too narrow.

Acol opening lead methods definitely have the edge here. Bridge players in the UK are taught from the very beginning to lead the Ace for attitude and the King for count in the suit. This method clearly has more frequency as well as wider application. In principle you can use it against suit contracts and no-trumps contracts alike.

So. we give up the ability to show precisely doubleton touching-honours but gain the flexibility of choosing whether we would like an attitude or count signal from partner.

In practice a King is led more often because it can be from top of a sequence or from a holding headed by Ace-King. Either way the count from partner immediately clarifies whether you can safely continue the suit or should switch to keep the tempo.

Facing your King lead the only exception for partner is to unblock a Queen or a Jack in the suit when defending no-trumps. In all other cases give your agreed count signal.

Your agreed count signal can of course be standard count (high-low for even number) or reverse count (upside-down count. low-high for even number). I prefer standard count.

When starting a high-low signal, because it may be too late by the second round, the first card should be as clear a high card as you can afford, normally the second highest card from four. From a doubleton containing an honour, partner will break the rule and play the small card (because dropping an honour in defending a suit contract must continue to mean that the next round of the suit is under control by ruff or by the lower touching honour).

An Ace lead of course does not necessarily promise the King. Occasionally we all lead an unsupported Ace to have a look around if we have nothing better to lead. From partner's point of view you may or may not have the King alongside (if you did then evidently a count request was not a priority). But either way partner must signal his attitude in the suit in the context of the dummy's holding. Naturally partner will indicate liking if he has the King himself but he also must be alert to signal positively when holding the Queen, so that the leader can now even underlead a King to put partner in. No additional damage is done by signalling the fact of the Queen if the declarer had the King all along when partner led his Ace in the first place.

Your attitude signalling method can again be standard attitude (high to indicate liking) or reverse attitude (upside-down attitude, low to show liking). I prefer reverse attitude.

17.2 Third-and-fifth leads against suit contracts

Third-and-fifth leads are the world standard (according to World Bridge Federation) against suit contracts, the standards being primarily determined by North American methods. It is not so common, for example, in some parts of Europe such as the UK, where it must clearly present an advantage for defenders against unfamiliar declarers.

In this system, when defending suit contracts the leader leads:

• The third highest card from an even number of cards other than a doubleton, and

• The lowest card from an odd number of cards.

So, the lowest card is led from 3 or 5 (or 7) cards and the third card is led from 4 or 6 cards (the top of a doubleton remaining the logical exception).

The above is the modern version of third-and-fifth leads. (In the original version the third highest card was the norm when holding 3 or 4 cards, the fifth with 5 or more cards). In fact the modern version could be more suitably called third-and-low.

So the third card is led both from 3 or 4 cards. This may sound inefficient but of course it is on a par with the ambiguity that the lead of a low card under the fourth-best (or second-and-fourth) system could turn out to be from a 3-card suit. At least in the third-and-fifth system partner knows immediately that the lead of the 2-spot card (or the lowest-spot card allowing for what partner can see in dummy and in his own hand) will always be either from 3 cards or 5 cards but never from 4 cards.

The second round of the suit resolves any remaining ambiguity. If the leader follows with a lower card (so, high-low) this shows an even number originally, whereas if the follow-on is a higher card (so, low-high) this shows an odd number originally, fitting in very nicely with the rest of their count signals for standard count giving partnerships. This also fits in with how doubletons are normally played on lead and altogether makes more sense from a count perspective than the fourth-best lead system (which would have had to lead low from 3 to an honour, still not resolving on the second round of the suit whether it was originally from 3 or 4 cards).

Third-and-fifth leads also seem to distinguish better for partner on the first round of the suit whether the lead is from a 4 card suit or a 5 card suit. When the fourth card is led in both scenarios in the fourth-best system, partner cannot read the lead as well especially if declarer is able to conceal low spot cards. But applying different lead criteria to neighbouring cases of 4 and 5 cards evidently enables better differentiation.

So, the overall merit of third-and-fifth leads as against the fourth-best leads is that the same lead principle (lowest or third) is applied to situations which are in fact two cards apart. If the lowest card is led from 3 or 5 card holdings (and the third card from 4 or 6 card holdings) this disparity of two cards gives partner more of a chance to read the actual holding immediately, given also the opponents' bidding.

Partner then applies the Rule of 10 or 12, for 5 card suits or 3 card suits, respectively, to establish the number of higher cards in declarer's hand (and often his precise holding by inference).

Knowing the count immediately is often more important in suit contracts so that partner can decide whether to cash winners before declarer can take discards, or to switch, etc.

One disadvantage of third-and-fifth leads is that the third card can sometimes be a fairly high spot, perhaps even the 8 or 9 spot, which may have been capable of promotion into a trick for the defence. In reality this may not be critical since the third round of a side suit is unlikely to stand up in a suit contract, but it may still be best to avoid leading from suits such as KJ92 or QT83 which likely gives away a trick or looks like a doubleton.

One other disadvantage, in fact more a culture shock than a disadvantage, is that the lead in the third-and-fifth system promises only the count in the suit but is entirely silent about whether or not the leader has an honour card in that suit. The idea here is that against suit contracts the count information is more important than attitude in the suit.

The fact that no honour card is promised in the suit when a relatively low card is led may well be anathema to most players brought up leading the fourth best away from an honour. But if the partnership can overcome this psychological hurdle for itself then the third-and-fifth leads in practice are more likely to trip up the declarer than the defence.

In fact the third-and-fifth leads fit well with a tight matchpoints style of avoiding leads from unsupported kings or queens as those are more likely to cost than gain, whereas a passive lead is usually more rewarding unless the auction suggested that the defence should be getting busy.

Third-and-fifth leads do not effect other lead agreements:

• Top of sequence leads remain as before

• Top of doubleton leads remain as before

• Top of nothing from three small cards if leader had raised partner in the suit

• King lead for count (unblock in no-trumps) and Ace/Queen lead for (reverse-) attitude

• Coded tens and nines still apply to both suit contracts and no-trump contracts

• Fourth best leads remain in place against no-trump contracts as before

17.3   Coded Nine and Ten leads

The principal idea here is that a lead of the 9-spot card or the 10-spot card shows either no higher card in the suit or two higher cards one of which will be immediate next card up. In contrast, leading the Jack denies any higher honours. (For this reason, the system is also known as 'Jack denies, 10 implies' although in our case I have also added the 9 into the mix.)

Other lead agreements are not affected and so everything else remains as before.

When a 9 or 10 card is led partner assumes that the leader has two higher cards unless the next higher card is in sight. If the leader advances the 10-spot and you are looking at the Jack in your own hand or in the dummy then obviously the leader had nothing higher. Similarly when the lead is the 9-spot but the 10-spot is also visible to you.

The system has the advantage of removing the ambiguity for the leader's partner about whether the lead was from top of a sequence with nothing higher or from an internal sequence with one non-touching higher honour. Admittedly the same deduction is available to the declarer, but the defence is usually better off having clear agreements even when this is shared.

Although primarily intended against no-trumps contracts, in the form presented here the coded 9 and 10 lead methods are equally applicable in defending suit contracts.

When it is the top of a sequence, it should be adequately backed up, such as T98x or at least T97x, so not just T9xx. This goes for any lead system, not only our Coded Nines and Tens system.

There are some exceptional holdings which do not fit well into this system (or most other systems). For example, against no-trumps, it would be better to lead the 9 from AKT93 or AQT94 to tell partner that you have at least got two higher cards, rather than lead the 10 which is likely to mislead partner into thinking that declarer must have all higher honours.

The system is not to be confused with 'Strong-Ten' leads because that system has implications not just for the Tens but also the Kings (whereas our King leads asks for count even when top of a sequence). Our Coded Tens and Nines methodology is also different from Journalist leads (in so far as the Ace-King combinations are concerned).

Chapter 18

Carding And Discarding

All players have their own preferences on carding and discarding methods. What follows is a summary of what I've grown to like for myself over the years and would wholeheartedly recommend to everyone.

18.1 Carding

Defending is more difficult than declaring in bridge not least because defence requires combining and co-ordinating your side's efforts between yourself and your partner.

Your primary tool for communicating with partner in defence is the card you choose to play in a suit when you do have a choice.

Obviously sometimes your choice is pre-determined in so far as you may need to cover declarer's or dummy's card or take your winner in the suit. In all other cases you will have a choice of cards to play whenever you have more than a singleton or an awkward doubleton.

Your carding on partner's opening lead should present no difficulty as this will have been discussed. Some partnerships choose to show nothing other than the count in the suit even here. I respect that this may be all some very exceptional players need because they are able to place all honour cards without help. For us mortals some help wouldn't go a miss and (unless partner specifically requested a count by leading the King) an attitude-defining signal on partner's opening lead is a valuable part of my game.

I like reverse-attitude signals (upside-down, low to show liking) mainly because a small card is more dispensable whereas a higher spot card may be a useful filler in later play.

Obviously the sight of the dummy might mean that the attitude of the follower (leader's partner) does not need further elucidation. For example. dummy may turn up solid in the suit or is set to win the trick cheaply anyway. In such cases where I am unable even to cover the dummy's card or otherwise just not contributing to the trick, as partner will discern. my carding switches to giving partner a count in the suit in case that helps.

As for a method to give count. I prefer the standard count signal (high to show even number and low to show odd number). All my other signalling methods are generally reversal or inversions and so maybe reverse-count would have been more consistent but I still prefer standard-count mainly for the reason that the second card in a 3-card holding may be too expensive as a signal because it may prove to be useful later.

The other obvious situation where not only an attitude signal but even a count signal would be redundant following partner's opening lead is when dummy turns out to be void in the suit, or has a singleton which you cannot beat, or even if partner is retaining the lead he will not be able to continue the suit profitably. If defending a suit contract my signalling priority now becomes giving a suit-preference to partner for his switch.

On suit-preference, I have a very strong liking for reverse-suit-preference (inverted Lavinthal). So a low card to show interest in the higher ranking of the remaining suits and a high card to show interest in the lower ranking of the remaining suits. This takes a little getting used to at first but once you are there it has an edge. It makes you think harder on each trick given that suit-preference has so many applications in defence.

In principle your lead and carding style at trick one is just as good when the defence has to open up a new suit in later play. But in practice you obviously must take into account the disclosed dummy and indeed the declarer's line of play up to that point, all of which means that you should really be breaking into a new suit with a much more incisive card.

During play, especially on declarer's or dummy's lead, there is no reason to give automatic count each time. Some counts help declarer more than they help the defence and so it needs to be done with discretion. This comes with experience but the main point is that you should give count only when you think partner may need it, such as when the declarer is trying to dislodge partner's stopper. If the fate of the suit is already determined one way or another then there is no point in giving count.

In practice the first defender to play to the trick. unless covering declarer's or dummy's card or taking a winner by choice or per force. has more reason to give count in case partner needs it to decide how to defend the suit. If the trick. and sometimes the fate of the entire suit. is already decided by the time the second defender is to play to the trick. then there is absolutely no point for that second defender to give count.

Not only is there no reason to give count but. more to the point. the choice of card by the second defender in those situations should be a (reverse) suit-preference signal for the next defensive move.

Especially when partner has won the trick ahead of you - at any stage of the defence - your card to follow suit should never be a lazy card but an obligatory (reverse) suit-preference card to direct partner's next move. Your only valid excuse for not giving a preference in these situations would be that you have only one card to play in the suit! If you have at least two cards to choose from. you have a preference to communicate.

18.2   Carding priorities

You need to have a flexible sense of priority about what message is the most relevant message that needs to be communicated to partner at each step of the defence. This is relevant not only on partner's initial lead but also in the rest of your carding in defence.

We already covered the position on partner's original lead: The first priority is (reverse) attitude. If that's already self-evident in the light of the dummy's holding in the suit. then there is no point in repeating your (reverse) attitude signal with your choice of card. In particular, there is no point in covering dummy's small or even intermediate card if you can only just beat it but your card is unlikely to dislodge an honour from declarer. In such situations you might as well move on to your next priority in your carding.

When a (reverse) attitude signal is redundant you need to be seamlessly moving in your thinking to your next priority, which should be a (standard) count in the suit. If that too is redundant then you need to be moving automatically to the next priority still, which should be a (reverse) suit-preference. All these changes of priorities should be pure reflex actions.

The same order of priority applies in later play too, except of course we omit the (reverse) attitude signal from our list of signal priorities altogether when it is not our partner leading to a trick. That's to say, an attitude signal is only relevant when partner is breaking a suit whether at trick one or in later play; attitude is not relevant when declarer or dummy is leading to a trick.

When declarer or dummy is leading to a trick during play, unless we are covering it or winning the trick, we now have a residual signalling priority list of only two. Your immediate priority now is give (standard) count if you think that will help partner in the suit - usually only if you are playing to the trick ahead of partner.

But if count is not relevant under the circumstances, maybe because partner has already won the trick ahead of you, then once again you move to your next priority signal, which is (reverse) suit-preference for partner's subsequent move.

So the full order of carding priority, subject to skipping what is no longer relevant at the given point in time for the defence is:

1. Reverse-attitude

2. Standard-count

3. Reverse-suit-preference

If you don't like my choices between the reverse and standard methods of giving any of these signals then decide what is best for you and what you feel comfortable with. But the point is that you must always have an order of priority in your carding so that partner knows what signal to expect when the normal signal is evidently not applicable under the circumstances.

18.3   Discards

Carding is when you are following suit; discarding is when you are not. The idea of a signal with your discard when you are not following suit is clearly a useful one. Some partnerships only give count in the suit discarded and so do not feel the need to give an attitude signal as to which of the remaining suits they rather like. I think that a direct signal to partner with your discard, especially if partner is taking the trick, cannot be a bad thing, if nothing else than to avoid disasters in cash-out situations.

I believe not only in having a discard method but actually having two methods. My idea here is that it can only be helpful to have one which acts as an overriding strong signal, in my case an odd-numbered card, and a somewhat lesser or secondary signal, in my case an even-numbered card.

All discards are of course suggestions to partner, rather than orders. But I think it is useful to have two methods to distinguish between the strengths of your message, of course only if the cards you happen to hold permit this distinction in the first place.

My preferred system is similar to the Italian system, sometimes called 'odds-and-evens', at least in so far as the odd cards are concerned. But with even cards, I again like to invert the suit-preference signal so that a higher spot card shows an interest in the lower ranking of the remaining two suits and a lower spot card shows an interest in the higher ranking of the remaining two suits.

All my suit-preference signals both in carding and discarding are reverse primarily for reasons of consistency. But it pays even more dividends to play reverse-suit-preference with discards because some self-assured declarers presume standard-suit-preference without bothering to look up my convention card or asking about our discards and I take particular pleasure when they go astray as a result of such disrespect to opponents.

The other merit of having two discard systems in one is that when you do not have, say, an odd card in the suit to discard with as a strong signal then you can still look for an appropriate even card in the other two suits to convey the message to partner. It may be a lesser signal with even cards but it is still some signal rather than none. Partner may even be able to work out that you can't have had your share of odd cards in the relevant suit.

Equally, depending on context, even cards are your closest way of giving no signal at all. I dislike methods where anything you discard apparently has to be saying something compelling.

Occasionally you just want to be able to say that you have no good cards to contribute to the defence or that you are somewhat neutral between the available options. An even card could carry that message of lack of urgency or preference, especially if your even-card message is for example seemingly showing enthusiasm for dummy's or declarer's strong suit.

But even when carrying no particular signal your even discards should still have some purpose. If you have nothing to say you can at least begin a count in the discard suit. If in the circumstances it couldn't possibly be showing the usual reverse-suit-preference for the indicated suit, then partner will read it as showing count in the discard suit instead.

One last point about discards concerns the subsequent count in the discard suit. If that suit had not been played before and so you had no occasion to begin giving a count, you should have a clear partnership agreement about the nature of count you now give in the suit in which, following your discard, you will have one fewer cards. Will your count be based on your original holding of the suit or your remaining holding?

I suggest the present standard-count in any depleted suit, so based on your remaining holding. This is easier and much more natural to relate to. This is the first time the suit is being played naturally and so your normal method of giving count should apply. Partner is aware about the card you already discarded.

18.4 Smith peters with a difference

It makes sense to play the same carding and discarding methods generally against both suit-contracts and no-trumps contracts - except for Smith which has a particular no-trumps rationale.

The idea with Smith peters is that, in defending no-trumps only, in the first new suit which declarer tackles after the initial lead, the original leader's partner, the follower, begins a peter (high-low) to confirm that he likes her original lead or plays low-high to show dislike. This is important when the follower's high card holding in the suit was not entirely clear from the card he played on partner's original lead of a small card in the suit.

This could happen when for example the follower contributes the Jack which loses to the declarer's King. If the leader has the Ace, then it is critical for her to know whether the follower or the declarer still holds the missing Queen.

If the leader gets-in during later play in a side suit, perhaps for the only time or at any rate before the follower could get in, without Smith she would not know whether the suit is ready to run or whether continuing the suit might set up the Queen for declarer.

But with Smith, the leader will have observed partner's attitude for her original lead from the way he follows suit to declarer's first suit, usually at trick 2. Holding the Queen he will have obviously showed liking, so leader can now cross to the Queen and the defence cash out their tricks in the suit. If partner had shown dislike then the leader will instead look for another entry in partner's hand, so that he can return the critical suit through declarer.

There are many situations like this when attitude about the lead could not have been communicated fully at trick 1 and so Smith solves it by a belated signal in another suit.

Obviously the leader's partner, the follower, may not have a free card to play on the first round of the suit declarer tackles on gaining the lead. For example, the follower may have to cover dummy's card instead of giving a Smith signal. In those situations the occasion for his Smith peter signal will be deferred until his first free card.

Smith peters definitely fulfil a role which normal carding methods cannot deal with. There is always a cost in terms of what we give up instead, in this case the count in the new suit. But that is a price well worth paying to clarify the position about the lead suit which in no-trumps is usually the best source of tricks for the defence.

When playing Smith, there should be a very clear partnership understanding that Smith always overrides any notion of giving count in the first suit declarer tackles. There is no choice.

The only exception for reverting to a count signal in the new suit would be if the declarer is trying to set up a suit in dummy which clearly has no side entry whatsoever and so the defence needs to know exactly how long to hold up their control card in the suit. Nothing else would do. If there is a possible side entry, then assume that it is an actual entry and still choose to give a Smith signal for the lead suit, not count in the present suit.

Smith peters are not only for the follower but also for the original leader - but to a limited extent and in a different sense. The leader should not have to worry about petering in the same way because it is fair to assume that she maintains an interest in the suit she chose to lead without having to reconfirm her liking. So she can defend normally against declarer's first suit.

On the contrary. I think that the original leader should only have to do the unusual. in our case give a Smith peter (play high on the first round of declarer's first suit) to *deny* continued interest in her own original choice of lead (maybe it was speculative and already failed). This reversal of signal when it comes to the leader of the suit herself makes a lot more sense to me than uniform Smith by both halves of the partnership.

So. I am suggesting one system but two different and opposite messages depending on who is giving the signal. Of course. in practice the follower's signal is the more critical one by far.

Convention Cards

Here you will find a choice of three ready-made convention cards:

- World Bridge Federation (WBF) convention card
- American Contract Bridge League (ACBL) convention card
- English Bridge Union (EBU) convention card

At the end you will also find supplementary notes which are common to all three convention cards. The WBF and EBU convention cards refer to the supplementary notes more specifically by note numbers. The ACBL card design does not particularly suit cross-referencing.

So, you can copy your choice of convention card plus the notes to form a complete system record and a summary of the entire book. Well, your partner needs a copy too.

OPENING	TICK IF ARTIFICIAL	MIN. NO. OF CARDS	NEG.DBL THRU	DESCRIPTION	RESPONSES	SUBSEQUENT ACTION	COMPETITIVE & PASSED HAND BIDDING
1♣	✓	2	3♠	10-20 HCP, 2-card suit / 4432	Transfers [1], Inverted raises [2]	See Notes [1,2,3,4]	Transfers OFF in competition [1] / Inverted raises ON in competition [2]
1♦		4	3♠	10-20 HCP	Weak jump shifts [4] / Inverted raises [2]	See Notes [2,3,4]	Inverted raises ON in competition [2]
1♥/♠		5	3♥	10-20 HCP	Weak jump shifts [4] / 2/1 G-F [5], 1NT 6-11 HCP [6], 2-tier splinters [9], Bergen [10], Jacoby [11]	See Notes [4,5,6,7,8,9,10,11]	Drury [7], Transfers over DBL [8] / Bergen/Jacoby variations [10,11]
1NT		1		15-17 HCP / 5M possible, 1-6m possible	2♣ Puppet [16,17] / 4-suit transfers [19,20]	See Notes [16,17,18,19,20,21,22,23]	Rubensohn [23] / System ON over DBL, RDL =m
2♣	✓			22+ HCP balanced OR strong 1/2/3-suited	Kokish style [27]	See Notes [27,28,29,30]	Opener's DBL/RDL = 22+
2♦	✓			Multi. Weak in a major OR 20-21 HCP balanced OR 18-21 HCP any 4441	2/3M Pass or correct	See Notes [29,30,31]	2NT rebid in competition = 2or3-suiter
2♥/♠	✓			Muiderberg, 6-10 HCP, 5 card Major & 4-card minor	2NT = ENQ, 3♠ = Pass or correct, / 3♦ = GF in opener's major	See Notes [32]	Responder's DBL = PEN / RDL = willing to play ♠ at 3-level
2NT	✓			Majors or Minors 5/5+, 6-10 HCP	3m = to play / 3♥ = ENQ / 3♦ = ENQ	See Notes [33]	Responder's DBL = PEN / RDL = single-suited hand
3♣		6		Natural, intermediate, 11-14 HCP	3M = Forcing, 5+ card suit	See Notes [12]	Responder's DBL = PEN / RDL = 6-card single-suited hand
3♦/♥/♠		6		Natural, pre-emptive			
3NT				Solid minor, little outside	4♣ = pass or correct		
4♣/♦		7		Natural, pre-emptive			
4♥/♠		7		Natural, pre-emptive			
4NT	✓			Specific Ace-ask	4♠ =none, 4NT= 2, 5♣ =♣A		
5♣/♦				Natural, pre-emptive			
5♥/♠				Natural, positional			

HIGH LEVEL BIDDING

Slam Methods:

RKCB	41 / 30 / 2-Q / 2+Q / Either/Or responses	See Notes [46,47,48]
Trump-queen ask, side-King ask	Step responses	See Notes [46,47,49,50]
Exclusion-RKCB	Step responses	See Notes [46,47,51,53,54]
Minor-suit RKCB	Step responses	See Notes [46,47,52,53,54]

SPECIAL DOUBLES

After Overcall: Penalty

Negative ☑ thru _____ 3♠

Responsive ☑ : thru _3♠_ Maximal ☐

Support: DBL ☑ thru _2♥_ Redbl

Card-showing ☐ Min. Offshape T/O ☐

SIMPLE OVERCALL

1 level _8_ to _____ HCP (usually)

often 4 cards ☐ very light style ☐

Responses

New Suit: Forcing ☑ NFConst ☐ NF ☐

Jump Raise: Forcing ☐ Inv. ☐ Weak ☑

JUMP OVERCALL

Strong ☐ Intermediate ☐ Weak ☑

OPENING PREEMPTS

	Sound	Light	Very Light
3/4 bids	☑	☑	☐

New Suit Forcing: 1 level ☐ 2 level ☑

DIRECT CUEBID

	OVER:	Minor	Major
Natural			
Strong T/O		☐	☐
Michaels		☐	☐

SLAM CONVENTIONS Gerber ☐ : 4NT: Blackwood ☐ RKC ☑ 1430 ☑

Minor suit RCKB, Exclusion RCKB

vs interference: DOPI ☐ DEPO ☐ Level: _____ ROPI ☐

LEADS (circle card led, if not in bold)

versus Suits	versus Notrump
X x x x Ⓧ x	X x x Ⓧ x x
x x x x x x x Ⓧ	x Ⓧ x x x x x
Ⓐ Ⓚ x Ⓣ 9 x	Ⓐ Ⓚ x Ⓙ Ⓣ x A Q J x
Ⓚ Ⓠ x K J Ⓣ x	A J Ⓣ 9 A T Ⓙ 9 x
Q J x K T Ⓣ 9 x	K Q J x Ⓚ Q T 9
J T 9 Q T Ⓣ 9 x	Q J T x Q T Ⓙ 9 x
Ⓚ Ⓠ T 9 J T 9 x	Ⓣ 9 x Ⓧ

LENGTH LEADS:

4th Best   vs SUITS ☐ vs NT ☑

3rd/5th Best   vs SUITS ☑ vs NT ☐

Attitude vs NT ☐

Primary signal to partner's leads

Attitude ☑ Count ☐ Suit preference ☐

SPECIAL CARDING ☑ PLEASE ASK

[Card design © 2008 ACBL Editor © 2009 CT]

NOTRUMP OVERCALLS

Direct: _15_ to _18_ Systems on ☑

Conv. ☐

Balancing: _11_ to _14_

Jump to 2NT: Minors ☐ 2 Lowest ☐

Conv. ☑ _2NT 2 lowest, weak or strong_

DEFENSE VS NOTRUMP

vs:		
2♣	transfers/showing	passed hand
2♣	show immediate	natural 5-10
2♦		natural 8-10
2♥		natural 5-10
2♠	show immediate	natural 8-10
Dbl:	penalty	majors 4-5
Other:	junior systems vs weak NT	

OVER OPP'S T/O DOUBLE

New Suit Forcing: 1 level ☐ 2 level ☑

Jump Shift: Forcing ☐ Inv. ☐ Weak ☑

Redouble implies no fit ☑

2NT Over: Limit+   Limit   Weak

Majors   ☑   ☐   ☐

Minors   ☐   ☑   ☐

Other: _TRF responses after 1M-(DBL)_

VS Opening Preempts Double is

Takeout ☑ thru _4♥_ Penalty ☐

Conv. Takeout ☐

Lebensohl 2NT Response ☑

Other

GENERAL APPROACH
2/1 GF

Two Over One: Game Forcing ☑ Game Forcing Except When Suit Rebid ☐

VERY LIGHT: Openings ☐ 3rd Hand ☑ Overcalls ☐ Preempts ☐

FORCING OPENING: 1♣ ☐ 2♣ ☑ Natural 2 Bids ☐ Other ☑ _2♦, 2NT_

NOTRUMP OPENING BIDS

1NT			
_15_ to _17_	3♣	natural and forcing	
	to	3♦	natural and forcing
5-card Major common ☑	3♥	natural and forcing	
System on over _DBL, 2♣_	3♠	natural and forcing	
2♣ Stayman ☐ Puppet ☑			
2♦ Transfer to ♥ ☑	4♦, 4♥ Transfer ☐		
Forcing Stayman ☐	Smolen ☐		
2♥ Transfer to ♠ ☑	Lebensohl ☐ (_____denies)		
2♠ TRF to 2♣	Neg. Double ☐		
2NT TRF to 3♣	Other: _Rubensohl_		

2NT	_____ to _____
Puppet Stayman ☐	
Transfer Responses:	
Jacoby ☐ Texas ☐	
3♠ _____ to _____	

3NT	_____ to _____

Conventional NT Openings

2NT weak minors or majors ☐

2NT gambling long minor ☐

MAJOR OPENING

Expected Min. Length	4	5
1st/2nd	☐	☑
3rd/4th	☑	☐

RESPONSES

Double Raise: Force ☐ Inv. ☐ Weak ☑

After Overcall: Force ☐ Inv. ☐ Weak ☑

Conv. Raise: 2NT ☑ 3NT ☐ Splinter ☑

Other: _TRF responses after DBL_

1NT: Forcing ☑ Semi-forcing ☑

2NT: Forcing ☑ Inv. ☐ _____ to _____

3NT: _____ to _____

Drury ☑ : Reverse ☐ 2-Way ☐ Fit ☐

Other:

MINOR OPENING

Expected Min. Length	4	3	0-2 Conv.
1♣	☐	☐	☑
1♦	☑	☐	☐

RESPONSES

Double Raise: Force ☐ Inv. ☐ Weak ☑

After Overcall: Force ☐ Inv. ☐ Weak ☑

Forcing Raise: J/S in other minor ☐

Single raise ☑ Other:

Frequently bypass 4+♦ ☐

1NT/1♣ _6_ to _10_

2NT Forcing ☐ Inv. ☑ _11_ to _12_

3NT: _13_ to _15_

Other: _TRF responses to 1♣_

DESCRIBE / RESPONSES/REBIDS

2♣	_22_ to _____ HCP		
Strong ☑ Other ☐		Kokish style	
2♦ Resp: Neg ☐ Waiting ☑			

2♦	_____ to _____ HCP	Multi	
Natural: Weak ☐ Intermediate ☐ Strong ☐ Conv. ☑		2NT Force ☑ New Suit NF ☐

2♥	_6_ to _10_ HCP	Muiderberg	
Natural: Weak ☑ Intermediate ☐ Strong ☐ Conv. ☑		2NT Force ☑ New Suit NF ☐

2♠	_6_ to _10_ HCP	Muiderberg	
Natural: Weak ☑ Intermediate ☐ Strong ☐ Conv. ☑		2NT Force ☑ New Suit NF ☐

OTHER CONV. CALLS: New Minor Forcing ☑ 2-Way NMF ☐

Weak Jump Shifts: In Comp. ☐ Not in Comp. ☐

4th Suit Forcing: 1 Rd. ☐ Game ☑

DEFENSIVE CARDING

	vs SUITS	vs NT
Standard:	☑	☑
Except ☑		
upside down suit-preference when count or attitude are not relevant		
Upside-Down:		
count	☐	☐
attitude	☑	☑

FIRST DISCARD

Lavinthal	☐	☐
Odd/Even	☑	☑
Even = U/D S/F	☑	☑

OTHER CARDING

Smith Echo		☑
Trump Suit Pref.	☐	
Foster Echo	☐	

GENERAL DESCRIPTION OF BIDDING METHODS

5 Card Majors, 15-17 No-Trump, 2/1 Game Force, Multi 2♦, Muiderberg 2M

1NT OPENINGS AND RESPONSES

Strength	15-17	
Shape constraints	5M or 6m possible	Tick if may have singleton ✔ minor
Responses	2♣ 5 card Puppet Stayman: Notes 16, 17, 18	

2♦	Transfer to hearts: Note 19	2♥	Transfer to spades: Note 19
2♠	Transfer to clubs: Note 20	2NT	Transfer to diamonds: Note 20
Others	See Notes 21, 22		

Action after opponents double	Systems 'ON'; XX = long minor (→ 2♣ = pass or correct to 2♦)
Action after other interference	Rubensohl: Note 23

TWO-LEVEL OPENINGS AND RESPONSES

	Meaning	Responses	Notes
2♣	22+ balanced/semi-balanced Or strong 1/ 2/ 3-suited hand	Kokish style	See Notes 27,28,29,30
2♦	Weak major or 20-21 balanced or 18-21 any 4-4-4-1 shape		See Notes 29,30,31
2♥	6-10 HCP, 5 ♥ and 4+ minor		See Note 32
2♠	6-10 HCP, 5 ♠ and 4+ minor		See Note 32
2NT	Minors or majors, weak, 5/5+		See Note 33

OTHER ASPECTS OF SYSTEM WHICH OPPONENTS SHOULD NOTE

(Please include details of any agreements involving bidding on significantly less than traditional values).

2-over-1 responses forcing to game (Note 5); 6-11 HCP 1NT response to 1M (Note 6); Transfer responses to 1♣ (Note 1); Transfer responses when our 1M is doubled (Note 8); Transfer advances following partner's overcall (Note 37); New Minor Forcing (Note 58); Also see Supplementary Notes

OTHER OPENING BIDS

	HCP	see Note	Min length	CONVENTIONAL MEANING	SPECIAL RESPONSES	Notes
1♣	10-20	✓	2		Transfers; inverted raises	1,2,3,4
1♦	10-20	✓	4		Inverted raises; 2M weak	2,3,4,5
1♥	10-20	✓	5		6-11 1NT, 2/1 GF; Bergen	4,5,6,7,8,9,10,11
1♠	10-20	✓	5		6-11 1NT, 2/1 GF; Bergen	5,6,7,8,9,10,11
3♣	11-14	✓	6	Intermediate 123		12
3♦♥♠	6+		6+	Pre-emptive		
3NT				Gambling		
4 bids	7+		7+	Pre-emptive		

DEFENSIVE METHODS AFTER OPPONENTS OPEN

NATURAL ONE OF A SUIT	CONVENTIONAL MEANING	SPECIAL RESPONSES	Notes
Simple overcall	5+ card suit, 8+ HCP	Transfers	37
Jump overcall	Weak 6+ card suit (but 3♣ Questem - Note 38)		38
Cue bid	Highest 2-suits, weak/strong		38
1NT Direct: Protective:	15-18 HCP 11-14 HCP	If doubled, bids=lower of 2-suits, XX=single-suited	
2NT Direct: Protective:	Lowest 2-suits, weak/strong 19-20 balanced	Systems 'ON'	38 29,30

OPPONENTS OPEN WITH	DEFENSIVE METHODS	SPECIAL RESPONSES	Notes
Strong 1♣	Truscott*ish* overcalls; weak jumps		39
Short 1♣/1♦	Initially treated as natural		
Weak 1NT	2♣=M or MM weak/strong; 2♦=MM 11-15 HCP	2♣-2♦ = ♠-preference	40
Strong 1NT	Same as above, see Note 40 for full system	Same as above	40
Weak 2	X=take-out; 2N=16-18; 4m = Leaping-Michaels	2N system on; Lebensohl	41,42
Weak 3	X=take-out; 4m = Non-leaping Michaels		41
4 bids	X = values; 4NT = 2-suited		
Multi 2♦	X =13-15 or 19+; 2NT=16-18; Leaping Michael	2N system on; Lebensohl	41,42

SLAM CONVENTIONS

Name	Meaning of Responses	Notes
RKCB	Composite 41 / 30 / 2-Q / 2+Q	46,47,48
Queen-ask, King-ask	Either/Or responses	46,47,49,50
Exclusion-RKCB	Step responses	46,47,51,53,54
Minor-suit RKCB	Step responses	46,47,52,53,54

COMPETITIVE AUCTIONS

Agreements after opening of one of a suit and overcall by opponents

Level to which negative doubles apply	Below 3NT generally
Special meaning of bids	5+ card responses except after 1♣-(1♦)
Exceptions / other agreements	See Notes 1,2,10

Agreements after opponents double for takeout

Redouble: 9+ HCP	New suit: Note 8	Jump in new suit: No change
Jump raise: Pre-empt	2NT: No change	Other:

Other agreements concerning doubles and redoubles

Support doubles/redoubles if both majors have been bid or implied; Game-try doubles; Responsive doubles; Lightner doubles; Doubling 3/6NT after one of us has shown a suit asks for a *different* lead

OTHER CONVENTIONS

See Supplementary Notes pages

SUPPLEMENTARY DETAILS

(Please cross-reference where appropriate to the relevant part of card, and continue on back if needed).

See Supplementary Notes pages

OPENING LEADS

Card led is highlighted in **bold**

3/5 leads vs Suit contracts						
A K	**A K** x	**K Q** 10	**K Q** x	**K** J **10**	K 10 **9**	**Q J** 10
Q J x	**J** 10 x	10 x **x**	**10** 9 x	**9** 8 7 x	10 x **x** x	H x **x**
H x x **x**	H x x x **x**	H x x x x **x**	**x** x	x x **x**	x x **x** x	

2/4 leads vs NT contracts						
A K x (x)	A J **10** x	**K Q** 10	**K Q** x	**K** J **10**	K 10 **9**	**Q J** 10
Q J x	**J** 10 x	10 x **x**	**10** 9 x	**9** 8 7 x	10 **x** x x	H x **x**
H x x **x**	H x x x **x**	H x x **x** x x	**x** x	x **x** x	x **x** x x	

Other agreements in leading, e.g. high level contracts, partnership suits:-

Top of nothing in partner's suit after raising it but normal lead with an honour;
From AK, KQ combinations, we lead K for count, A or Q for reverse-attitude
Coded 9s and 10s: normally, either no higher card or 2 higher cards including the next one up

CARDING METHODS

	Primary method v. suit contracts	Primary method v. NT contracts
On Partner's lead	Reverse attitude (Standard count)	Reverse attitude (Standard count)
On Declarer lead	Standard count (optional)	Smith and reverse-Smith – see below
When discarding	Odd=enc; Even=reverse suit preference	Odd=enc; Even=reverse suit preference

Other carding agreements, *including secondary methods (state when applicable) and exceptions to above*

Carding priority order: reverse-attitude, standard-count, reverse-suit-preference;
'Present' count in depleted suits;
In NT-defence: Smith by original-leader's-partner (High likes) but reverse-Smith by leader (Low likes);

SUPPLEMENTARY DETAILS (continued)

See Supplementary Notes pages

1.   Transfer responses to 1♣ opening bid

All responses up to and including 2NT are transfers to the next strain
Transfers remain 'ON' after first opponent's intervening double but 'OFF' after overcall

1♣- 1♦*	Shows 4+ hearts, 6+ HCP (natural 1♦ is not available)
1♣- 1♥*	Shows 4+ spades, 6+ HCP
1♣- 1♠*	6-10 or 16+ HCP balanced, denies 4+ card major
1♣- 1N*	Inverted ♣-raise, 5+ cards, 10+ HCP (but natural-NT after overcall)
1♣- 2♣*/2♦*/2♥*	3-way transfers to next strain (but 2♣ inverted ♣-raise after overcall)
1♣- 2♠*	11-12 HCP balanced, denies 4+ card major, maybe 3-3-3-4 shape
1♣- 2N*	8-9 HCP inverted raise (but natural balanced 11 HCP after overcall)
1♣- 3♣	6-7 HCP inverted raise (but 6-9 HCP inverted ♣-raise after overcall)

If next opponent passes, opener's completion of transfer shows weak hand with poor-fit;
Opener resumes normal rebid with all 15+ HCP hands or with 2+ card fit in 12-14 hands

If next opponent doubles or overcalls transfer-request, opener's rebid options include:

1♣-(P/X)-1♥*-(X)-P					No voluntary bid or completion, 12-14 HCP, 0-2 spades
→	→	→	→	XX	Support redouble with 3 spades, 15+ HCP
→	→	→	→	1♠	Voluntary completion, 3-cards (again) but here 12-14 HCP
→	→	→	→	1N	15+ HCP voluntary bid with ♥-stopper(s), maybe 1-3-4-5 shape
→	→	→	→	2♣	Natural, 5+ clubs, 12+ HCP, not 3 spades
→	→	→	→	2♦	Reverse, forcing
→	→	→	→	2♥	15+ HCP cue bid of "opponent's suit", multi-purpose force
→	→	→	→	2♠	12-14 HCP with 4 spades, a "jump" raise
→	→	→	→	2N	18-19 HCP after opponent's double with ♥-stopper(s)

1♣-(P/X)-1♦*-(X)-P					No voluntary bid or completion, 12-14 HCP, 0-2 hearts
→	→	→	→	XX	Negative redouble, 4 spades *and* 3 hearts
→	→	→	→	1♥	Voluntary completion, 3 hearts, 12-14 (15) HCP
‚	→	→	→	1♠	4+ card spade suit (again) but here denying 3 hearts
→	→	→	→	1N	15+ HCP voluntary bid with ♦-stopper(s), maybe 3-1-4-5 shape
→	→	→	→	2♣	Natural, 5+ clubs, 12+ HCP, not 3 hearts, not 4 spades
→	→	→	→	2♦	15+ HCP cue bid of "opponent's suit", multi-purpose force
→	→	→	→	2♥	12-14 HCP with 4 hearts, a "jump" raise
→	→	→	→	2♠	Reverse, forcing
→	→	→	→	2N	18-19 HCP after opponent's double with ♦-stopper(s)

1♣-(P/X)-1♦*-(1♠)-P					No voluntary bid or completion, 12-14 HCP, 0-2 hearts
→	→	→	→	X	Support double with 3 hearts, 12+ HCP, unlimited
→	→	→	→	1N	15+ HCP (not 12-14) with ♠-stopper(s), not 3 hearts
→	→	→	→	2♣	Natural, 5+ clubs, 12+ HCP, not 3 hearts
→	→	→	→	2♦	Reverse, forcing
→	→	→	→	2♥	12-14 HCP with 4 hearts, a "jump" raise
→	→	→	→	2♠	15+ HCP cue bid of opponent's suit, multi-purpose force
→	→	→	→	2N	18-19 HCP after opponent's double with ♠-stopper(s)

2.   Minor suit inverted raises and other responses

1♣ (overcall)-2♣	Inverted ♣-raise, 5+ cards, 10+ HCP (still inverted after overcall)
1♣-(pass)-1N*	Transfer ♣-raise, 5+ cards, 10+ HCP (transfer-raise if no overcall)
1♣-1N*-2♣	Simple completion showing only 2-card club suit, 12-14 HCP
→ → 2other	3+ clubs, stop in suit shown, no stop if bypassed, 12+ HCP
→ → 2NT	Opener has exact 14 HCP, 3+ clubs
→ → 3♣	5+ clubs, not forward-going
→ → 3NT	18-19 HCP
→ 2N*	8-9 HCP, 5+cards ♣-raise (but natural 11 HCP after overcall)
→ 3♣	6-7 HCP, 5+cards raise (but 6-9 HCP raise after overcall)
→ 3♦/♥/♠	12-15 HCP, splinter raise in clubs, denies a 4 card major

1♦- 2♦	10+ HCP and 4+card raise, also applies after intervention
→ → 2♥	Opener has heart-stop (but does not deny spade-stop), 12+ HCP
→ → 2♥ 2♠	Opener has heart-stop, responder confirms spade-stop
→ → 2♥ 2NT	Opener has heart-stop, responder has probable spade-stop
→ → 2♠	Opener has spade-stop and denies heart-stop
→ → 2NT	Opener has exact 14 HCP
→ → 3♦	5+ diamonds, not forward-going
→ → 3NT	18-19 HCP
→ 2NT	11-12 HCP balanced, probably no 4-card major
→ 3♣	8-9 HCP and 4+card ♦-raise, also applies after intervention
→ 3♦	6-7 HCP and 4+card raise, also applies after intervention
→ 3♥/3♠/4♣	12-15 HCP, splinter raise in diamonds, denies a 4 card major

1♦- 2♦- (2M)-P	Opener's pass shows weak-NT hand
→ → → → X	Responder's double reconvenes our sequence

1m-3N	Natural, 12-15 HCP, to play, usually 3-3-3-4 or 3-3-4-3
1m-4m	Minor-suit RKCB (→ see Note: Minor-suit RKCB)

3.   Impossible major as good raise of minor

Responder's rebid of a previously denied major is a good raise of the opener's minor

1♣-1♠*-2♦	Responder transfers to 1NT and opener reverses
→ → → 2♥	Good raise in ♣ (having denied a ♥-suit already)
→ → → 2♠	Good raise in ♦ (having denied a ♠-suit already)
→ → → 3♣	Weak raise in ♣
→ → → 3♦	Weak raise in ♦

1♣-1♠*- 2♥	Responder transfers to 1NT and opener reverses
→ → → 2♠	Good raise in ♣ (having denied a ♠-suit already)
→ → → 3♣	Weak raise in ♣

1♥- 1N-2♦	Opener replies in NT and opener rebids a lower-rank suit
→ → → 2♠	Good raise in ♦ (having denied a ♠-suit already)
→ → → 3♦	Weak raise in ♦

4.   Weak jump shifts

Weak jump shifts also apply over opponent's double:

1♣- 2any   See Note: Transfer responses to 1♣
1♦- 2M   5-8 HCP, 6 card suit (including the sequence 1♦-(1♥)-2♠)
1♥- 2♠   5-8 HCP, 6 card suit
Note: 1M response and then 2M (rather than jump-shift) would be 9-10 HCP, 6-card suit

Opener may continue responder's jump-shift with a regular Ogust enquiry:

2NT   Strong enquiry
→ 3♣   Lower range, with 1 of top 3 honours
→ 3♦   Lower range, with 2 of top 3 honours
→ 3♥   Higher range, with 1 of top 3 honours
→ 3♠   Higher range, with 2 of top 3 honours
→ 3NT   AKxxxx in the anchor suit

5.   2-over-1 Game-Force responses

A 2/1 response (1M-2x or 1♦-2♣) is forcing to game, with certain exceptions

The exceptions are:
- If responder is a passed-hand (if opener opened in 3rd or 4th seat)
- If first opponent overcalls (when responder's bids revert to normal)
- If first opponent doubles our 1♦ (when responder's bids revert to normal)
- If first opponent doubles our 1M (when we play tranfer responses → see Note)
- If only a minor suit fit emerges (when we may not bid the hand to the 5-level)
- If responder rebids his minor (invitational, 6+ card suit, 10-11 HCP)

1M-2m-2M   Unbalanced, no extras, not necessarily a 6th card in the major
1♣- 2♥- 3♥   Shows extras as well as fit

6.   6-11 HCP 1NT response to 1M

A 1NT response by an unpassed responder to a 1M opening bid shows:
- 6-11 HCP
- No 4-card spade suit in response to hearts
- No 4+card support for opener's major - see Note 10
- No 3-card support for opener's major - except specifically in a 10-11 HCP hand

The system is off (the 1NT response is not forcing but natural):
- If responder is a passed-hand (if opener opened in 3rd or 4th seat)
- If first opponent overcalls (when responder's bids revert to normal)
- If first opponent doubles our 1M (when we play transfer responses → see Note 8)

7.   Drury

2♣ passed-hand response to a 3rd/4th seat 1M opening bid is artificial, showing
- 3 or 4-card support for opener's major; and
- Maximum passed-hand values (invitational hand including distributional values)

In reply, the opener describes his hand:
- 2M rebid is bare minimum (11-12 HCP)
- 2♦ is artificial and shows sound opening bid (13-14 HCP) but no particular extras
- 2♥ (after 1♠-2♣) shows sound opening bid (13-14 HCP) with 4-card heart suit
- Rebids higher than 2M show extra values and/or shape and are invitational
- 2NT is 14 HCP balanced
- 3NT is 18-19 HCP balanced

8.   Transfer responses when our 1M opening bid is doubled

1♥- (X)-1♠	This one is *not* a transfer: Shows 4+ spades, 6+ HCP (normal bid)
→ → 1N*	Shows 6+ clubs in weak hand or 4+ clubs in good hand
→ → 2♣*	Shows 6+ diamonds in weak hand or 5+ diamonds in good hand
→ → 2♦*	Shows a good raise to 2♥, about 7-9 HCP, 3 card support
→ → 2♥*	Shows a weak raise to 2♥, about 4-6 HCP, 3 card support
1♠- (X)-1N*	Shows 6+ clubs in weak hand or 4+ clubs in good hand
→ → 2♣*	Shows 6+ diamonds in weak hand or 4+ diamonds in good hand
→ → 2♦*	Shows 6+ hearts in weak hand or 5+ hearts in good hand
→ → 2♥*	Shows a good raise to 2♠, about 7-9 HCP, 3 card support
→ → 2♠*	Shows a weak raise to 2♠, about 4-6 HCP, 3 card support

Transfer responses start from 1NT (no natural 1NT when opponent doubles our 1M)
Pass, redouble and higher level responses retain their usual meanings, 2NT is Jacoby
Transfers into another suit at 2-level could be a 6+ card suit in only a 7+ HCP hand
Opener's completion of transfer does not imply fit, only denies big opening hand
Responder's belated 2M is usually Hx; 3M is 3-card invitational; cue-bid is stop-asking

9.   Two-tiered splinter system over partner's 1M

1♥- 3N/4♣/4♦	13-14 pure HCP with splinter in ♠/♣/♦
1♥- 3♠	11-12 HCP with unspecified splinter
→ → 3N	Name your splinter (→ 3♥ reply acts as proxy for ♠ splinter)
1♠- 4♣/♦/♥	13-14 pure splinter as named
1♠- 3N	11-12 HCP with unspecified splinter
→ → 3♣	Name your splinter (→ 3♠ reply acts as proxy for ♣ splinter)

10.   Bergen*ish* sequences

1M-2M	6-9 HCP, 3 card support (if doubled → see Note 8: Transfer responses)
1M-2NT	Jacoby GF with 4+ card support (→ see Note 11: Jacoby sequences)
1M-3♣	10-11 HCP with 4+ card support
1M-3♦	7-9 HCP with 4+ card support
1M-3M	Pre-emptive 4+ card support

If opponent overcalls:

1M-(overcall)-2M	Weak raise with 3 card support
1M-(overcall)-3M	Weak raise with 4 card support
1M-(overcall)-Cue	Good raise or better with 3 card support
1M-(overcall)-2NT	Good raise or better with 4+ card support
1M-(overcall)-3NT	To play, with less than 3 card support

Passed-hand Bergen and other responses:

P-1M-1NT	6-9 HCP, natural, denying 3-card support
P-1M-2♣	Artificial, 3 or 4-card raise, 10-11 HCP (→ see Note 7: Drury)
P-1M-2M	6-9 HCP, 3-card raise
P-1M-3♣	7-9 HCP with 4+ card support (passed-hand Bergen shift down one bid)
P-1M-2NT	Natural 11 HCP

11.   1M-2NT Jacoby*ish* sequences

1M-2NT	Jacoby: game forcing raise with 4+ card support
→ → 3M	6th card in Major, better than minimum
→ → 3other	4+ card side suit, better than minimum
→ → 3NT	18-19 balanced
→ → 4M	Minimum
→ → 4other	Splinter (does not promise extra values)

12.   Intermediate 3♣ opening bid

3♣	Intermediate opening bid, 11-14 HCP, 6 card suit
→ 3♦	Enquiry with ♣Hxx or better, inviting 3NT with 2 of 3 top honours
→ → 3♥	1 of top 3 honours, lower range, 11-12 HCP,
→ → 3♠	1 of top 3 honours, higher range, 13-14 HCP,
→ → 3N	2 of top 3 honours, irrespective of HCP-count
→ 3M	5+card suit, forcing
3♣- (X)-XX	Invitational with a major

Note: Other 3-level openings (3♦, 3♥, 3♠) remain normal pre-empts

16.   1NT-2♣ Puppet Stayman sequences

Quantitative raise to 2NT goes through 2♣ (so 2♣ does not promise a major)
With 4-4 in majors, over opener's 2♦, the responder bids 2♥ showing ♠

1NT					15-17; 5-card Major or 1-6 card minor possible, not 2/2 M/M
→	2♣				Puppet Stayman, constructive, at least good-7 to 8
→	→	2♦			Opener has at least one 4-card Major, no 5-card Major
→	→	→	2♥		Responder has 4 spades, may also have 4 hearts
→	→	→	→	2♠	Opener agrees spades; 15-16 HCP
→	→	→	→	3♠	Opener agrees spades; 17 HCP
→	→	→	→	2NT	Opener denies spades (must have 4 hearts); 15-16 HCP
→	→	→	→	3NT	Opener denies spades (must have 4 hearts); 17 HCP
→	→	→	2♠		Responder has 4 hearts, denies 4 spades
→	→	→	→	2NT	Opener denies 4 hearts (must have 4 spades); 15-16 HCP
→	→	→	→	3NT	Opener denies 4 hearts (must have 4 spades); 17 HCP
→	→	→	→	3♥	Opener agrees hearts; 15-16 HCP
→	→	→	→	4♥	Opener agrees hearts; 17 HCP

1N-2♣-2M				Opener has 5 card major
→	→	→	4NT	Quantitative (other-M then 4NT would be RKCB in opener's M)
→	→	2NT		Opener has no 4 or 5 card major; 15-16 HCP
→	→	→	3m	To play, responder had longer minor with a 4 card major
→	→	→	3M	GF, 5 card major plus 4+ other major (will bid on with 5/5)
→	→	→	4m	MSRKCB for minor
→	→	3m		No 4 or 5 card major but this 4+ card minor and 17 HCP
→	→	→	3M	GF, 5 card major plus 4+ other major (will bid on with 5/5)
→	→	→	4m	MSRKCB for minor

1N-2♣- any-3m	5-card minor, forcing

After opener's Stayman-reply shows a 5-card major responder's 4NT is still quantitative;
To set opener's major for RKCB the responder inserts other major before bidding 4NT;
This manoeuvre does not apply if opener replied 2♦ originally. So only in the following:

1N-2♣- 2♥- 2♠- any- 4NT   becomes RKCB for hearts (cancelling the earlier 2♠), and
1N-2♣- 2♠- 3♥- any- 4NT   becomes RKCB for spades (cancelling the earlier 3♥ bid).

Similarly after Puppet-Stayman over 2NT, a level higher, following a 2NT-3♣-3M start

17.   **When opponents double our 2♣ Stayman bid**, we play:

* Pass shows club stop(s) (→ redouble from partner reconvenes Stayman)
* 2♦ denies a club stop and confirms at least one 4-card major
* 2M denies a club stop and shows a 5 card major

18.   **When opponents overcall our 1NT with 2♣ natural** (or 2-suited with clubs)

* Double = Stayman
* In all other respects, our system remains 'ON' including transfers

19.   **Breaking major suit transfers over 1NT**

* 3M = 15-16 HCP and 4-card support
* Other suit = poor doubleton, 17 HCP and 4-card support; (2NT = no poor doubleton)
* 4M = 15-16 HCP and 5-card support
* 3NT = 17 HCP and 5-card support

20.   **Minor suit transfers over 1NT**

* 1NT-2♠ is a transfer to clubs; 1NT-2NT is a transfer to diamonds; 6-card suit
* Completing minor suit transfers *shows* Axx, Kxx, Qxx or better fit (for 3NT);
* Short-breaking minor suit transfers to the intermediate step *denies* such fit;
* With both minors and weak, transferor bids 2NT for ♦ and passes any 3♣ reply
* Responder's 2nd round bid = shortage

21.   **Responder's options with both major suits over partner's 1NT**

With weak 4/5 or 5/4	Transfer to 5-card major to play (no 'garbage-Stayman')
With weak 5-5	Either transfer to better major or treat as invitational 4/5
With invitational 4/5	Transfer to hearts and rebid spades, keeping to 2-level
With invitational 5/4	Start with 2♣; pass any 2N reply; over 3m bid 3♠ showing 5/4
With invitational 5/5	Transfer to spades and rebid hearts at 3-level, non-forcing
With game-going 4/5	Start with 2♣; over 2N or 3m reply bid 3♥ showing 4/5+ forcing
With game-going 5/4	Start with 2♣; over 2N or 3m reply bid 3♠ showing 5/4+ forcing
With game-going 5/5	Start with 2♣; over 2N or 3m reply bid 3♠ forcing (and rebid 4♥)

22.   Other 1NT sequences

1N- 2♥- 2♠- 3m	Responder's new suit at 3-level = F1
1N- 2♥- 2♠- 4N	Quantitative with 5 spades
1N- 3M	Slam try in Major (opener cues to agree, bids 3NT to discourage)
1N- 3M-3N- 4N	RKCB in Major (opener overruled, responder in charge)
1N- 3m	Slam-try in minor (opener cues to agree, bids 3NT to discourage)
1N- 3m-3N- 4m	MSRKCB in minor (opener overruled, responder in charge)
1N- 2N- 3m-4♣	5+/5+ in minors, MSRKCB based on ♣ (may later still declare in ♦)
1N- 4♣	Gerber
1N- 4M	Natural, to play
1N- 4N	Quantitative
1N- 2♣- 2♥- 2♠- any- 4NT	RKCB for hearts (4N cancels responder's earlier 2♠ bid)
1N- 2♣- 2♠- 3♥- any- 4NT	RKCB for spades (4N cancels responder's earlier 3♥ bid)

23.   Rubensohl

When opponents overcall our 1NT opening bid, our responder's options are:

→ X	Penalty
→ 2-level suit bids	4+ suit, to play
→ 2N and 3-level suit bids below rank of oppo suit	Transfer to 5+ suit any strength
→ Cue or 3-level suit bids above rank of oppo suit	Transfer to 5+ suit invitational +
→ 3-level transfer to opponent's suit	Asking, Staymanic, game-force
→ 3NT	Denies major(s), shows stop

Fast arrival shows stopper (FASS)
Same methods generally when overcall was conventional but indicated an anchor suit

27.   Kokish style sequences

2♣						22+ HCP balanced or strong 1/2/3-suited hand
→	2♦					Relay
→	→	2♥				Artificial – usually 2-suited hand → see sequences further below
→	→	2♠				Artificial – any 3-suited GF hand → see sequences further below
→	→	2NT				22-23 HCP balanced or semi-balanced → Note: 2NT Sequences
→	→	3♣				Single-suited ♣ GF (→ next suit up = 0-1 fit; other = cue, 2+card fit)
→	→	3♦				Single-suited ♦ GF (→ next suit up = 0-1 fit; other = cue, 2+card fit)
→	→	3♥				Single-suited ♥ GF (→ next suit up = 0-1 fit; other = cue, 2+card fit)
→	→	3♠				Single-suited ♠ GF (→ next suit up = 0-1 fit; other = cue, 2+card fit)
→	→	3NT				26+ balanced or semi-balanced

2♣	2♦	2♥				Artificial, seeking further relay
→	→	→	2♠			Relay
→	→	→	→	2N		24-25 HCP balanced or semi-balanced
→	→	→	→	3♣		2-suited, ♣ and a Major
→	→	→	→	→	3♦	Identify your major
→	→	→	→	→	other	Cue-bid, with ♣ set as trumps
→	→	→	→	3♦		2-suited, ♦ and ♥
→	→	→	→	→	3♥	Sets ♥
→	→	→	→	→	other	Cue-bid, with ♦ set as trumps
→	→	→	→	3♥		2-suited, ♥ and ♠
→	→	→	→	→	3♠	Sets ♠
→	→	→	→	→	other	Cue-bid, with ♥ as trumps
→	→	→	→	3♠		2-suited, ♠ and ♦
→	→	→	→	→	4♦	Sets ♦
→	→	→	→	→	other	Cue-bid, with ♠ as trumps
→	→	→	→	3N		2-suited, minors
→	→	→	→	→	4m	Responder's better minor

2♣	2♦	2♠			Artificial, 3-suited, 22+ HCP, any 4-4-4-1 or 5-4-4-0 shape
→	→	→	2N		Relay
→	→	→	→	3♣	3-suited hand with singleton or void ♣
→	→	→	→	3♦	3-suited hand with singleton or void ♦
→	→	→	→	3♥	3-suited hand with singleton or void ♥
→	→	→	→	3♠	3-suited hand with singleton or void ♠

28.   When opponents intervene with our 2♣ opening bid

- Opener's re-opening double or redouble = 22+ fairly balanced
- Opener's re-opening 2NT rebid = 2-suited (or 3-suited) hand
- Opener's re-opening suit-rebid = natural one suited or not-balanced
- Responder's free bid over intervening double or bid is natural and value-showing

29.   2NT sequences via 2♣, 2♦, etc

2NT		20-21 via 2♦, 22-23 via 2♣-2♦-2NT, 24-25 via 2♣-2♦-2♥-2♣-2NT, etc
→	3♣	5-card Puppet Stayman (→ see Note: Puppet Stayman)
→	3♦	Transfer to ♥
→	3♥	Transfer to ♠
→	3♠	Slam-try in either minor, promising 5/4+
→ →	4m	Choosing 4+ card minor suit but not keen on slam
→ →	4♥	Step-RKCB for ♣
→ →	4♠	Step-RKCB for ♦
→	3NT	To play (probably without a 3-card major)
→	4♣	Slam-try in ♥ (→ 4♦ = co-operative; 4♥ = sign-off; 4N = RKCB in ♥)
→	4♦	Slam-try in ♠ (→ 4♥ = co-operative; 4♠ = sign-off; 4N = RKCB in ♠)
→	4♥	Slam-try in ♣ (→ 4♠ = co-operative; 4N = to play; 5♣ = sign-off)
→	4♠	Slam-try in ♦ (→ 4N = to play; 5♣ = co-operative; 5♦ = sign-off)
→	4NT	Quantitative (probably without a 3-card major)

30.   2NT-3♣ Puppet Stayman sequences

With invitational hand of 5 spades and 4 hearts, responder still starts with 3♣
With 5-4 or 4-4 in the majors, over opener's 3♦, the responder bids 3♥ showing ♠

2N 3♣					5-card Puppet Stayman
→	→	3♦			Opener has at least one 4-card major or 3 spades
→	→	→	3♥		Responder has 4 or 5 spades, may also have 4 hearts
→	→	→	→	3♠	Opener has 4 hearts, denies 4 spades
→	→	→	→	3NT	Opener has 3 spades, denies 4 hearts
→	→	→	3♠		Responder has 4 hearts, denies 4 spades
→	→	→	3NT		Responder has no 4 card major (was checking for 5)
→	→	→	4NT		Quantitative (having checked for any 5 card major first)
→	→	3♥			Opener has 5 hearts
→	→	→	3♠		Responder has 4 spades (OR prelude to RKCB in hearts)
→	→	→	4NT		Quantitative (other-M then 4NT would be RKCB in opener's M)
→	→	3♠			Opener has 5 spades
→	→	→	4NT		Quantitative (other-M then 4NT would be RKCB in opener's M)
→	→	3NT			Opener has neither 3+ spades nor 4+ hearts
→	→	→	4NT		Quantitative (having checked any major fit first)

After opener's Stayman-reply shows a 5-card major responder's 4NT is still quantitative;
To set opener's major for RKCB the responder inserts other major before bidding 4NT;
This manoeuvre does not apply if opener replied 3♦ originally. So only in the following:

2N 3♣ 3♥ 3♠ any 4NT   becomes RKCB for hearts (cancelling the earlier 3♠), and
2N 3♣ 3♠ 4♥ 4♠ 4NT   becomes RKCB for spades (cancelling the earlier 4♥ bid).

Similarly after Puppet-Stayman over 1NT, a level lower, following a 1NT-2♣-2M start

31.   **Multi 2♦ sequences**

2♦			6-10 HCP in a major Or 20-21 balanced Or 18-21 HCP any 4-4-4-1
→ 2M			Pass or correct
→ → 2NT			Opener reveals 20-21 hand type → See Note: 2NT Sequences
→ → 3any			18-21 HCP, 4-4-4-1 with singleton shown (but 2♦-2♠-3NT is ♥-singleton)

2♦ 2N			Responder's strong enquiry
→ → 3♣			6-8 HCP weak-2 in ♥
→ → → 3♦	Asking about top-3 ♥-honours (→ 3♥ = 0-1; 3♠ = 2 of the top 3)
→ → 3♦			6-8 HCP weak-2 in ♠
→ → → 3♥	Asking about top-3 ♠-honours (→ 3♠ = 0-1; 3N = 2 of the top 3)
→ → 3♥			9-10 HCP weak-2 in ♥
→ → 3♠			9-10 HCP weak-2 in ♠
→ → 3N			AKQxxx in a major
→ → 4any			18-21 HCP, 4-4-4-1 with singleton as shown

2♦ 3M			Pass or correct, with 3+ cards in both majors
→ → 3NT			Opener reveals 20-21 hand type (or 18-21 HCP any 4-4-4-1 hand)
→ → → 4♣	4-card Stayman (→ 2♦-3M-3NT-4♣-4♦-4NT is to play)
→ → 4M			Opener had 20-21 hand-type with the 5-card major as shown

2♦ 4♣			Asking opener to *transfer* to his M (so, responder plays it)
→ 4♦			Asking opener to *bid* his M (so, opener still plays it)
→ 4M			To play, responder has single-suited hand of his own

When opponents overcall or double our multi 2♦:
- Responder replies generally similarly (2NT is still an enquiry but 3NT is to play)
- Responder's redouble shows willingness to compete to 3-level in spades only
- Responder's double of opponents' suit overcalls are for penalties (even at 2-level)

32.   **Muiderberg 2M sequences**

2M		6-10 HCP, 5 card Major as bid and a 4+ card minor
→ 2NT		Enquiry
→ → 3m		Poor 5/4 hand with the minor shown
→ → 3♥		Good 5/4+ hand with ♣
→ → 3♠		Good 5/4+ hand with ♦
→ 3♣		Pass or correct
→ 3♦		Sets partner's major as trumps and is GF
→ → 3M		A void somewhere (→ next-step asks where)
→ → 3other	Singleton
→ → 3NT		2-2 shape alongside 5-card Major and 4-card minor

When opponents overcall or double our Muiderberg 2M:
- Responder replies generally similarly (2NT is still an enquiry but 3NT is to play)
- Responder's redouble = single-suited (→ opener bids next step for pass-or-correct)
- Responder's double of opponents' suit overcalls are for penalties (even at 2-level)

33.   Unusual 2NT opening bid (in Level 4-5 events only)

2N	6-10 HCP, either majors or minors, 5/5+
→ 3m	Responder's better minor, to play if opener has mm
→ 3♥	Strong enquiry (→ opener bids 3♠ with MM. 3NT with mm)
→ 3♠/4m/4M	To pass or correct to the lower ranking of the right 2-suits
→ 3N	To play

When opponents overcall or double our 2NT opening bid:
- Response system remains ON (3♥ is still an enquiry; 3NT is to play), except that:
- Responder's double of opponents' overcalls are for penalties
- 2NT-(X)-Pass = responder has no 3-card minor
- 2NT-(X)-XX = responder has own 6+ suit (→ opener bids 3♣ as pass-or-correct)
- After 2NT-(P/X)-3♣-(P), opener's 3♦ = good-MM, 3♥ = poor-MM
- After 2NT-(P/X)-3♣-(X), opener's pass = mm, 3♦ = good-MM, 3♥ = poor-MM
- After 2NT-(P/X)-3♥*-(X), opener's pass = MM, 3♠ = good-mm. 3N = poor-mm

Level 3 variation: We play 2NT openers as minors-only in Level 3 events

37.   Transfer advances following partner's overcall of opponent's opening bid

Our advancer uses transfers only for suits bypassed by partner's overcall. For example:

(1♦)-1♠-(P)-1N	Natural (1NT by advancer remains natural)
→ → → 2♣	Natural (because overcaller did not bypass clubs)
→ → → 2♦*	Shows hearts, indeterminate values
→ → → 2♥*	Good transfer raise to 2♠ with 3 card support
→ → → 2♠*	Weaker or distributional raise with 3 card support
→ → → 3♠*	Distributional raise with 4 card support

(1♠)-2♥-(P)-2♠*	Shows clubs, indeterminate values
→ → → 2N	Natural (lowest-NT bid by advancer remains natural)
→ → → 3♣*	Shows diamonds, indeterminate values
→ → → 3♦*	Good transfer raise to 3♥ with 4 card support
→ → → 3♥*	Weaker or distributional raise with 4 card support

System remains 'ON' if second opponent passes or bids 1NT or negative-doubles
System is 'OFF' if second opponent raises opener's suit or introduces new suit
Overcaller's completion of transfer does not imply fit, only denies very big overcall hand
Advancer may pass overcaller's completion of transfer or bid next feature of hand

38.   Questem (inverted Ghestem) 2-suited overcalls

Our 2-suited overcalls are 5-5 shape and either weak (6-10 HCP) or strong (16+ HCP)

- Cue bid of opponent's suit   Highest ranking two suits
- 2NT jump overcall   Lowest ranking two suits
- 3♣ jump overcall   Highest and lowest suits
- No strong option available in a 3♣ jump overcall when one of the two suits is clubs

(1m)-P/X-(1♥)-2♥ or similar sequence is natural (not a 2-suited overcall)

39.   Truscott*ish* overcalls of opponents' strong-1♣ opening bid or 1♦ relay

All jump overcalls are weak with 6 card suit
All non-jump overcalls are 2-suited, 5/4+ either way, indeterminate strength:

(1♣)-X	Clubs and hearts
→ 1♦	Diamonds and hearts
→ 1♥	Hearts and spades
→ 1♠	Spades and clubs
→ 1N	Diamonds and spades
→ 2♣	Clubs and diamonds
→ 2♦/♥/♠	Weak, 6 card suit

(1♣)-P-(1♦)-X	Diamonds and spades
→ → → 1♥	Hearts and spades
→ → → 1♠	Spades and clubs
→ → → 1N	Clubs and hearts
→ → → 2♣	Clubs and diamonds
→ → → 2♦	Diamonds and hearts
→ → → 2M	Weak, 6 card suit

40.   Overcalling opponents' 1NT opening bid

(1N)-2♣	One or both majors, either weak or strong
(1N)-2♦	Both majors, 4/4 or better, intermediate
(1N)-2♥/♠	Natural, 5+ cards, intermediate

Same system against weak or strong NT but with discretion as to relative vulnerability
Same system in both direct and protective overcall positions but the latter can be lighter

(1N)-2♣	One major (6 cards) or both majors (4/4+), either 6-10 or 16+ HCP
→ → 2♦	Advancer prefers ♠ (3+ cards), or is 2-1-5-5, not forward-going
→ → 2♥	Advancer prefers ♥ (3+) or equal-length MM or 1-2-5-5, not forward-going
→ → 2♦/♥-3♥/♠	Overcaller reveals the 16+ HCP overcall hand, 6-card major
→ → 2♦/♥-2NT	16+ HCP, both majors, 4/4+, not suitable for double originally
→ → 2♠	Pass or correct; perhaps game-going if overcaller owns up to hearts
→ → 2N	Advancer's strong all-purpose general enquiry
→ → → 3♣	6-8 HCP, one or both majors (→ 3♦ = advancer prefers ♠, 3♥ = ♥)
→ → → 3♦	9-10 HCP, both majors, 4/4+
→ → → 3♥/♠	9-10 HCP, 6-card major
→ → P	Advancer weak with 6/7 clubs and no 2-card major
→ → 3♣	Advancer weak with 6/5+ minors and no 2-card M, pass or correct
→ → 3♦	Advancer weak with 6/7 diamonds and no 2-card major
→ → 3♥/♠	Advancer invitational one-suited in major, 0-1 cards in other major
→ → 2♦- 2♥- 2♠	No-fit; Advancer weak with 5-6 spades, 0-1 hearts, not forward-going
→ → → → 2N	No-fit: Advancer has 0-1 hearts but 5/5 in minors, pick one, non-forcing
→ → → → 3m	No-fit: Advancer has 0-1 hearts and this 6-card minor, not forward-going
→ → 2♥- 2♠- 2N	No-fit: Advancer has 0-1 spades but 5/5 in minors, pick one, non-forcing
→ → → → 3m	No-fit: Advancer has 0-1 spades and this 6-card minor, not forward-going
→ → → → 3♥	No-fit: Advancer has 0-1 spades and 6-7 hearts, not forward-going

If 2♣ is doubled then advancer bids 2♦/♥ with 2-card differential preference, else passes;
If double reaches overcaller: 2M=6-cards; 2♦= 4/4 M/M; XX=5/4 (→2♦ asks for longer M)

(1N)-2♦	Both majors, 4/4+, intermediate, 11-15 HCP
→ → 2N	Enquiry (→ Ogust range and longer-Major replies over 4 steps)
→ → → 3♣/♦	11-13 HCP, ♣ for longer (or equal) hearts, ♦ for longer spades
→ → → 3♥/♠	14-15 HCP, ♥ for longer (or equal) hearts, ♠ for longer spades

If 2♦ is doubled then advancer bids 2♥/♠ with 2-card differential preference, else passes;
If double reaches overcaller: 2M = longer major; XX = equal length in majors

(1N)-2♥/♠	5+ cards in major, intermediate 11-15 HCP, essentially natural
→ → 2N	Enquiry (→ Ogust range and honours responses over 4 steps)
→ → → 3♣/♦	11-13 HCP, ♣ for 1 of top-3 honours, ♦ for 2 honours in major
→ → → 3♥/♠	14-15 HCP, ♥ for 1 of top-3 honours, ♠ for 2 honours in major

(1N)-X	Seeking penalty, 15-18 HCP
(1N)-2N	5-5+ in minors with 11-15 HCP, OR any 2-suiter with 16+ HCP
(1N)-3any	Pre-emptive 6+ card suit

Passed-hand overcalls of opponent's 1NT opening bid:

2♣/♦	6 card minor suit, natural, 8-10 HCP
2♥/♠	5 card major suit, natural, 8-10 (11) HCP
X	5/4 M/M either way (→2♦ by advancer says no preference)

41.   Leaping and Non-Leaping Michaels 4♣ or 4♦

Our jump overcall to 4♣ or 4♦ over opponent's weak-2 opening or our non-jump overcall of 4♣ or 4♦ over their 3-level pre-emptive opening shows a strong two-suited hand:

(2M)-4m	The minor shown plus the other major
(3m)-4m cue bid	Both majors
(3♣)-4♦	♦+M (→ 4♥: pass-or-correct)
(3♦)-4♣	♣+M (→ 4♦: which major?)
(3M)-4m	The minor shown plus the other major

Also applicable against opponents' two-suited and other weak 2 or 3-level openings:

- Over Lucas and Muiderberg 2s: treat their anchor suit as weak pre-empt
- Over Multi-2♦: 4♣ = ♣+M (→ 4♦: which major?); 4♦ = ♦+M (→ 4♥: pass-or-correct)
- Over weak-2♦: 4♣ = ♣+M (→ 4♦: which major?); 4♦ = both majors

42.   Lebensohl FASS

When partner doubles opponents' weak-2, multi-2♦ and similar bids, we play:

→ 2-level suit bid	4+ suit, to play, 0-7 HCP
→ 2NT	Relay to 3♣, pass-or-correct to another below their suit, to play
→ 3-level suit bids below opponent's suit	4+ suit, invitational, 8-11 HCP
→ 3-level cue bid	Staymanic, 4 cards in other/both major(s)
→ 3-level suit bid above opponent's suit	5+ suit, forcing if direct, invitational via 2N
→ 3NT	No 4 card/other major, with stopper if direct, no stopper via 2N

We play Lebensohl in all the following situations:

- In (2M)-X-(P)-2NT where opponent's 2M was a weak-major;
- In 1♥-(2♠)-P-(P)-X-(P)-2NT where opponent's 2♠ was a weak jump
- In (1M)-P-(2M)-X-(P)-2NT where partner doubles their raise to 2M
- In (1M)-X-(2M)-P-X-(P)-2NT where partner repeat-doubles their 2M sign-off
- In (1M)-P-(2M)-P-(P)-X-(P)-2NT where partner protects over their 1M-2M sign-off
- Generally when opponent(s) open/bid-up-to 2M and partner doubles for takeout

45.   5NT Grand Slam Force or Pick-A-Slam

With a known/implied major suit fit, 5NT is a GSF asking about the top 3 honours only:

- 6-level below trumps   None of the top 3 honours
- 6-trumps   1 of the top 3 honours
- 7-trumps   2 of the top 3 honours

Without a known fit, or after 3-suits, or if opponents compete, 5NT is a pick-a-slam bid

46.   Our Roman Key Card Blackwood matrix

Version	Starter	Reply	Q-ask	Reply	K-ask	Reply
Regular RKCB	4NT	composite	next	either/or	5NT	either/or
Exclusion-RKCB	5x	steps	next	steps	next	steps
Minor-suit RKCB	4m	steps	next	steps	next	steps

47.   When opponents interfere with our RKCB asking bids

- Pass   = First step reply of our applicable system
- Double/Redouble   = Second step reply of our applicable system
- Next step over intervention = Third step reply of our applicable system
- Second next step   = Fourth step reply of our applicable system, and so on
- Same principles whether the asking bid was for key cards or trump-Q or side-Kings
- We ignore opponent's doubles of our *responses*

48.   RKCB sequences: when responder has a void in regular RKCB only

Exception response in regular RKCB instead of the system 41/30 etc response:

4N- 5NT	2 key cards plus a working void (not in partner's first suit)
→ 6 other below trumps	1 or 3 key cards plus void in the named suit
→ 6 trumps	1 or 3 key cards plus void in a higher-ranking suit

Responder does not attempt to show a void if he has no key cards at all

49.   Either/Or responses to trump-Queen enquiry in regular RKCB only

If initial key card reply was 41/30 the next non-trump step asks for trump-Queen:

→ Lowest-level trump sign-off	No trump-Queen (and no information about side-Kings)
→ 5NT	Trump-Queen but no side-King
→ Other-suits bids	Trump-Q plus **either** named King **or** both other Kings

Note: Enquirer needs to hold one side-King of his own (or be prepared to play in 6NT) in case responder's reply carries the bidding beyond 6-level of the intended trump suit

50.   Either/Or responses to side-Kings enquiry in regular RKCB only

After initial key card reply (and maybe also after Queen-ask and negative reply) 5NT confirms that all 5 key cards are present and asks for side-Kings:

→ 6 of agreed trump suit	No side-Kings
→ Other-suit bids	**either** the named side-King **or** both other side-Kings

Note: Enquirer needs to hold one side-King of his own (or be prepared to play in 6NT) in case responder's reply carries the bidding beyond 6-level of the intended trump suit

51.   **Exclusion-RKCB sequences: when enquirer has a void**

- Splinter+1 level jump in a suit shows void and starts RKCB excluding that suit
- Exclusion-suit can be an unbid suit or the opponents' suit (but not partner's suit)
- If done prior to suit agreement then last naturally bid suit is presumed trumps
- Key card replies are based on 3 working Aces plus the trump-King (4 key cards)
- *All* key card replies are in non-composite steps (including 4/5NT): 0,1,2,3,4
- Enquirer may follow with trump-queen enquiry (→ See Note: Step responses)
- And/or side-Kings enquiry excluding void suit King (→ See Note: Step responses)
- Random start point in Exclusion-RKCB (usually 5x) and so step replies *throughout*
- When replying to Exclusion, the responder does not try to show any void of his own

52.   **Minor-suit RKCB (MSRKCB)**

- A *clearly* forward-going 4m bid is a speculative slam-try, asking for key cards
- Key card replies are in non-composite steps: 0,1,2,3,4 (including 4NT/5m)
- Following initial key card response, initiator may sign off in 2 ways: in 4NT or 5m
- Any follow-on enquiry excludes 4N and 5m as active steps for the enquirer
- Enquirer may follow with trump-queen enquiry (→ See Notes: Step responses)
- And/or side-Kings enquiry (→ See Notes: Step responses)
- Variable start point in MSRKCB (4♣ or 4♦) and so step replies *throughout*
- When replying to MSRKCB, the responder does not attempt to show a void

53.   **Step-responses to trump-Queen enquiry** in Exclusion-RKCB and MSRKCB

In MSRKCB 4NT and 5m are *not* available as asking steps for enquirer. Subject to that:
Next forcing step following key card reply asks: Do you have the trump-Queen?

→ Step 1 reply	No trump-Queen
→ Step 2 reply	Trump-Queen but no side-King
→ Step 3 reply	Trump-Queen plus 1 side-King
→ Step 4 reply	Trump-Queen plus 2 side-Kings
→ Step 5 reply (in MSRKCB only)	Trump-Queen plus 3 side-Kings

54.   **Step-responses to side-Kings enquiry** in Exclusion-RKCB and MSRKCB only

The asking bid for side Kings ("next forcing step") could be either of the following:

- Next non-trump step following trump queen enquiry and reply; or
- Second non-trump step following the initial key card reply (i.e. skipping Q-enquiry)

So, the next forcing step asks: How many side Kings do you have?

→ Step 1 reply	No side Kings
→ Step 2 reply	1 side-King
→ Step 3 reply	2 side-Kings
→ Step 4 reply (in MSRKCB only)	3 side-Kings

58.   New Minor Forcing over lowest-NT rebid (12-14) and jump-NT rebid (18-19)

Over opener's NT rebid a previously unbid minor by responder is an artificial asking bid
Opener's reply shows range and major-suit length/fit (♥-reply does not deny ♠-feature)
System applies similarly over opener's 2NT's rebid, non-jump still 12-14 or jump 18-19
Responder's rebid of opener's opening minor (or jump to other minor) is weak to play

Sample New Minor Forcing sequences following opener's 1NT rebid (12-14):

1♣-1♦*-1NT-2♣	Natural to play (NB ♣ was 2+ cards and ♦-reply showed ♥)
1♣-1♦*-1NT-2♦	New Minor Forcing (♣ was 2+ cards and ♦-reply showed ♥)
→ → → → 2♥	Minimum, 3-card heart-fit, may still have 4 spades if 4-3-3-3
→ → → → → 2♠	Responder is 4-4 in majors and minimum for NMF (11 HCP)
→ → → → 2♠	Opener minimum with 4 spades, not 3 hearts, 4234 or 4225
→ → → → 2NT	Minimum 12-13 HCP, no feature in majors, 3244/3235/2245
→ → → → 3♣	Maximum 14, no feature in majors, 3235 or 2245
→ → → → 3♥/♠	Maximum 14 with shown major feature (3♥ does not deny ♠)

1♦-1♠-1NT-2♦	Natural to play, responder unbalanced, spades + diamonds
1♦-1♠-1NT-2♣	New Minor Forcing (11+ HCP)
→ → → → 2♥	Minimum 12-13 HCP, 4 hearts, may still have 3 spades
→ → → → → 2♠	Responder has 5 spades, not 4 hearts, minimum for NMF
→ → → → 2♠	Opener minimum 12-13 HCP, 3-card spade-fit, not 4 hearts
→ → → → 2♦	Minimum 12-13 HCP, no feature in majors, 2353/2344/2254
→ → → → 2NT	Maximum 14 HCP, no feature in majors, 2-3-4-4 shape
→ → → → 3♣/♦	Maximum 14 HCP, no feature in majors, 3♣:2254, 3♦:2353
→ → → → 3♥/♠	Maximum 14 with shown major feature (3♥ does not deny ♠)

Following NMF enquiry and opener's response:
• Responder's 2NT if available is a sign-off
• Responder's 2♠ over opener's 2♥ is a 'pass or correct-to-2NT'
• Responder's raise to 3 of the major last bid by opener is strong, 4M is fast-arrival

If responder spurns NMF altogether:
1m-1M; 1NT-2m   Natural to play in opener's minor (having checked a Major)
1m-1M; 1NT-3om   Jump in other minor is natural, weak, does not seek correction

If opponent's double our NMF asking bid of 2♣, 2♦, 3♣, or 3♦, then we play that:
• Pass shows stop(s) in that minor (→ redouble from partner reconvenes our bidding)
• Redouble denies a stop in the minor and also denies anything to add in the majors
• Ignoring the double to show range and majors feature denies a stop in the minor

59.   "Serious 3NT"

In 2/1 sequences and without competition, after 3-level major suit agreement (even if by preference), the next bid (whether by opener or responder) indicates suitability for slam:

- 3NT   "Serious 3NT", slam-going hand in the Major, demanding a cue-bid;
- 4x below-M   Courtesy cue-bids promising no extras (so not serious about slam);
- 4M   Absolutely minimum

60.   When opponents double our Fourth-Suit-Forcing bid

- Pass shows stop(s) in fourth-suit (→ redouble from partner reconvenes our bidding)
- Redouble denies a stop in fourth-suit and also denies extra shape
- Rebidding a suit shows extra shape and denies a stop in fourth-suit

61.   Switched meanings of pass and double when opponents cue-bid our suit

- We switch the meanings of double and pass when opponents cue bid our suit
- Applies to our first bid after an opponent cue bids our earlier naturally bid suit
- Also applies to opponents' cue-bid (but not to their natural rebid attempts) of our 1♣
- Also applies to opponents' other artificial rebids of our suit, even during their RKCB

Exceptions:
- Support double/redouble override
- When opponent's cue bid shows 2-suited hand (→ Note: 2-suited overcall defence)

62.   When opponents make a 2-suited overcall

If their 2-suited overcall specifies both their suits, then:

- Cue of the cheaper of their suits = good raise in partner's suit
- Whereas, a direct raise of partner's suit = weak/fair raise
- Cue of their other suit = 5+ cards in 4th suit, forcing
- Whereas, a direct bid of 4th suit = non-forcing, competitive
- X = Penalty for at least one of their suits (partner bids on if weak or distributional)

If their 2-suited overcall shows one anchor suit and an unspecified second suit, then:

- Cue of their anchor suit = good raise of partner's suit
- Whereas, a direct raise of partner's suit = weak/fair raise
- Direct bid of new suit = forcing, especially if it is a major
- X = competitive, interest in other suits, tolerance for partner's suit rebid

63.   Responder's 2NT rebid as game-force after major-suit agreement

Opener may raise responder's major on 3 cards (usually with weak side suit doubleton);
Applies equally to "jump" completion of a transfer response following a 1♣ opening bid;
After 2-level major suit agreement, responder's new suit is game-try, 2NT is game-force

1m- 1M- 2M- 2N	Game-force with major suit agreement
→ → → → 3♣	3-card raise warning with minimum hand (12-13 HCP)
→ → → → 3♦	3-card raise warning but with values to spare (14-15 HCP)
→ → → → 4M	4-card fit, minimum (fast arrival), maybe no shortage
→ → → → 3M	4-card fit, maximum, maybe no shortage
→ → → → other	4-card fit, two-tiered splinter or semi-solid first suit indicator

All 'other' opener rebids between 3M and 4M are splinter or semi-solid suit as follows:-
Two-tiered splinter bids akin to those in Note 9 but with tiers now as 12-13 and 14-15;
Exception: Impossible splinter (opener's first suit) is now semi-solid suit source of tricks

August 2015 © TK